T012653?

ANALECTA ROMANICA

HERAUSGEGEBEN VON FRITZ SCHALK

unter Mitwirkung von Horst Baader (Köln), Yvon Belaval (Paris),
Herbert Dieckmann (Ithaca), Hugo Friedrich (Freiburg), Wido Hempel
(Hamburg) und Erich Loos (Berlin).

Heft 32

VITTORIO KLOSTERMANN · FRANKFURT AM MAIN

WILLIAM TRAPNELL

VOLTAIRE AND HIS PORTABLE DICTIONARY

VITTORIO KLOSTERMANN · FRANKFURT AM MAIN

© Vittorio Klostermann Frankfurt am Main 1972
Alle Rechte, auch das der Übersetzung vorbehalten
Herstellung: Universitätsbuchdruckerei Junge & Sohn, Erlangen
Printed in Germany

Voltaire's *Dictionnaire philosophique* presents an enigma for the uninitiated, because it is neither a dictionary nor a work of philosophy according to modern definitions of these terms [1]. It owes the noun in its title to the alphabetical order of its essays and the adjective to an eighteenth-century connotation of the word meaning free thought or thought free of traditional religious authority [2]. Stigmatizing such "superstition" as the "infamous" [3] in his correspondence with other "philosophers", Voltaire urged them to "crush" it in the famous slogan *Ecr. l'Inf.* which closed his letters to them. His determination to destroy this enemy, which absorbed the last third of a long life, produced many volumes of polemical literature and at least one great book, the *Dictionnaire philosophique portatif*. Far more compact than Bayle's *Dictionnaire historique et critique* (1697) and the *Encyclopédie ou Dictionnaire raisonné* (1751—1765) edited by Diderot, it fully deserved the epithet *portatif* included in the original title. Yet it surpassed the other two great alphabetical works of the Enlightenment in militance, cunning, daring and energy.

Voltaire's portable dictionary was the first in a series of alphabetical publications by him, each of which swallowed the preceding one like Breughel's fish: *le Dictionnaire philosophique portatif* (1764,

---

[1] In his preface to a 1962 edition of the work (Paris: Club Français du Livre), Yves Florenne makes the same point: "Ce n'est pas le trait le moins singulier ni, à tout prendre, le moindre mérite du *Dictionnaire philosophique* que de n'être ni philosophique, ni dictionnaire. Qu'est-ce, en effet, qu'un dictionnaire de cent mots? Pas même un lexique, tout au plus une liste où l'ordre alphabétique est bien moins un classement qu'un artifice, un jeu, un appât. Et déguisé en dictionnaire ... il ne l'est guère, ni dans l'esprit, ni dans la lettre".

[2] But not religion in general: "Voltaire ... thought of himself as the prophet of a new, universal religion, a kind of minimum creed, acceptable to all reasonable men. And for all his ferocious attacks on clerical intolerance, bigotry and fanaticism, Voltaire had no desire to see the priesthood abolished. In the *Dictionnaire philosophique* and elsewhere, he makes it clear that priests have an important function in his ideal society." Ronald Ridgeway, "Voltaire as an Actor," *Eighteenth-Century Studies*, I, 276.

[3] Voltaire's use of the word *infâme*, which varies in precision and meaning, has inspired many critical interpretations. Theodore Besterman's may be the most comprehensive of them all: "anything from clerical superstition to organized religion." *Voltaire's Correspondence*, no. 7584, note 7. Henceforth such references will read Best. 7584n7.

1764 [4], 1765, 1767), *la Raison par alphabet* (1769) and *Questions sur l'Encyclopédie* (1770—1772, 1774), to mention only original editions and those in which he revised, rewrote, expanded, replaced or eliminated existing articles and added new ones. His revisions of and additions to articles included in the *Questions* are so substantial that one may consider this work a separate one. Voltaire also contributed articles to the *Encyclopédie ou Dictionnaire raisonné* and definitions to the dictionary (in the modern sense) of the French Academy. Together with all of these alphabetical works, the editors of the posthumous Kehl edition of complete works (1794—1787) inherited from him a manuscript entitled *Opinion en alphabet*. Instead of separating these works, as one might expect, they grouped them in an alphabetical "cornucopia" [5] with extraneous writings, among them the *Lettres philosophiques* (1734). This they called *le Dictionnaire philosophique*!

In his edition of Voltaire's *Oeuvres complètes* (1828—1840) Adrien Beuchot cleaned house somewhat by placing the *Lettres* and other independent works in the *Mélanges*. But he did not sort out the definitions written for the Academy dictionary, nor did he try to disentangle the rest of the alphabetical jungle in Kehl. He did designate the origins of the items he found there. Louis Moland as usual reproduced Beuchot, including the title *Dictionnaire philosophique*, in his edition of Voltaire's complete works (1877—1885). Not until 1935 did Raymond Naves extract all the material that can be logically placed under this title. His text [6] includes the contents of the important editions published between 1764 and 1769 as well as revisions of and additions to articles continued in the *Questions*. Under the direction of Jérôme Vercruysse a team of scholars are presently working on critical editions of all the alphabetical writings for the forthcoming *Complete Works*. They will finally sort out the separate titles, producing several volumes of largely neglected material [7].

But the present study is concerned with the *Dictionnaire philosophique portatif* alone, from its conception at Potsdam in 1752 until the last edition of the three-word title to be sponsored by Vol-

---

[4] Postdated 1765.

[5] Besterman, *Voltaire* (New York, 1969), p. 435.

[6] Variants and notes by Julien Benda. I will refer to the 1967 re-edition (Paris: Garnier).

[7] Vercruysse discusses this project in "les Oeuvres alphabétiques de Voltaire", *Revue de l'Université de Bruxelles*, XXII (1969—1970), pp. 89—98.

taire, in 1767. Since his long "coquetterie" [8] with the Encyclopedia complicated the development of the work, this aspect of the story must also be taken into consideration. Needless to say, he was concentrating on the propagation of free thought and the destruction of religious authority during all of this period. Most of the works he was writing and the dictionary in particular were weapons in this war, which he looked upon as both total and holy. He devoted not only his publications, but also his correspondence to the dissemination of "philosophy". This commitment inspired many of his quarrels, his campaigns to redress judicial errors and even his administration of Ferney. The richest source of information about all of these activities is of course his correspondence, in which frequent allusions to the *Portatif* can usually be dated. To be sure, he seldom ran the risk of unguarded sincerity in his letters, but rather apportioned to each correspondent a measure of truth consistent with his trust in him. Nevertheless, comparison of letters with each other or other documents allows a fairly accurate determination of certain basic facts: when Voltaire was preoccupied with the *Portatif*, when he was working on it, what his intentions in writing it were, how successful he thought he was in carrying them out, how dangerous he considered his enemies' reactions to the work, what he did to counter them and how satisfied he was with the results. The answers to these questions should eclucidate the all-important relationship between such a man and such a work.

Long before he actually began to compose a philisophical dictionary, he had been writing the kind of articles that would eventually characterize his alphabetical works. As René Pomeau indicates in "Histoire d'une oeuvre" [9], Voltaire first published "Gloire" (1741) and "Déisme" (1742) in his *Mélanges* and later, in the *Questions* where he re-entitled the latter piece "Théisme". Elsewhere, Pomeau also notes Voltaire's studies in Biblical criticism in collaboration with his mistress Mme. du Châtelet during the Cirey period (1736—1741). "A Berlin", concludes Pomeau, "Voltaire rédigera très vite les articles *Abraham*, *Baptême*, *Moïse*: il est évident qu'il disposait alors de matériaux accumulés durant la période de Cirey" [10]. After weighing the same evidence, Ira Wade describes the development of the dictionary form as a progression from independent essays to complementary articles. "Voltaire undertook the writing of the dictionary articles", he states, "before he had the idea of assembling them in

---

[8] Naves, *Voltaire et l'Encyclopédie* (Paris, 1938), p. 1.

[9] *L'Information littéraire*, VII (1955), pp. 43—50.

[10] *La Religion de Voltaire* (Paris, 1956), pp. 173—174.

dictionary form ... He began to publish [them] just about the time plans were being laid to publish an encyclopedia (1743)" [11]. Wade remarks that Voltaire was as usual abreast of his times. Alphabetical compilations specializing in various subjects were in fact beginning to proliferate, but only Bayle's great *Dictionnaire* seems to have impressed Voltaire at the moment, although he frequently criticized even this work as cumbersome.

On 25 August 1752, during his stay at the court of Frederick II in Potsdam, he wrote his publisher Conrad Walther in Dresden, asking for a copy of Bayle's dictionary. The earliest evidence that he was thinking of a "philosophical dictionary" of his own occurred shortly thereafter. To Frederick, who was reviewing his troops in Silesia, he wrote on September 5: "Nous avons de beaux projets pour l'avancement de la raison humaine" (Best. 4383). Both Besterman and Koser-Droysen [12] suggest that this vague sentence refers to the dictionary, which Voltaire would, in fact, have considered a project for the advancement of human reason. But his secretary Cosimo Collini is more explicit in reporting one of Frederick's fabled dinner parties that took place on September 28: "On s'était amusé de l'idée d'un dictionnaire philosophique ... cette idée s'était convertie en un projet sérieusement adopté ... les gens de lettres du roi lui-même devaient y travailler de concert et ... l'on en distribuerait les articles, tels que *Adam, Abraham,* etc. ... Voltaire, vif et ardent au travail, commença dès le lendemain" [13].

In a letter to his friend the countess Bentinck that same day he asked for Calmet's works of Biblical erudition [14], which he would both exploit and ridicule in the *Portatif* [15]. He repeated this request

---

[11] "The Genesis of the *Questions sur l'Encyclopédie*" in *The Search for a New Voltaire, Transactions of the American Philosophical Society,* XLVIII, Part 4 (1958), p. 83.

[12] Reinhold Koser and Hans Droysen, *Briefwechsel Friedrichs des Großen mit Voltaire* in *Publikationen aus den K. Preußischen Staatsarchiven,* LXXXI—LXXXII (Leipzig, 1908).

[13] *Mon Séjour auprès de Voltaire* (Paris, 1807), pp. 32—33.

[14] *Dictionnaire historique, critique ... de la Bible* (Paris, 1720—1721) and *Commentaire littéral sur ... l'ancien et [sur le] nouveau testament* (Paris, 1707—1716).

[15] "Calmet was singled out by Voltaire because he was a contemporary and because his commentary on the Bible was considered the definitive religious view; which in reality it was not ... Whatever the picture of Calmet which emerges from Voltaire's allusions to him, we are constrained to note that no other writer supplies Voltaire with more information on scripture." Arnold Ages," Voltaire, Calmet and the Old Testament," *Studies on Voltaire and the Eighteenth Century* (or *SVEC*), XLI, 88.

in other letters to her on October 2 and 3. On October 3 he also told his close friend the comte d'Argental that his poetic inspiration had abandoned him: "Je compile à présent" (Best. 4406). He was certainly working on his dictionary. If his earlier remark to Frederick was indeed an allusion to this project, he must have conceived it himself, shared it with friends and then brought it up at the dinner party, or at least supported it strongly.

The Encyclopedia, in which he was beginning to take an interest [16], may have inspired the thought of directing such a collective enterprise. Just that summer the Prades affair [17] had confirmed him in the belief, which had brought him to Potsdam in the first place, that "philosophical" warfare must be waged from foreign soil. On October 20 his correspondent Wilhelmine, margravine of Bayreuth, wrote her brother Frederick as follows: "Il y a quelques gens de lettres qui sous la direction de Voltaire travaillent à un *Dictionnaire de raison*... je me suis engagée à faire quelques articles de ce Dictionnaire" [18]. Nothing seems to have come of this collaboration, however, for no articles by the margravine or any of Voltaire's colleagues in the Berlin Academy have, to my knowledge, ever appeared in the *Portatif* or elsewhere in his alphabetical works.

Nevertheless, it seems safe to assume that he himself spent the month of October working on the dictionary. Sometime in October-November a spirited exchange of letters between Frederick upstairs and Voltaire downstairs in the Sans Souci Palace [19] indicates that the latter had already made considerable progress. In Best. 4427 Frederick

---

[16] Early in 1752 Voltaire had included a "Catalogue des écrivains" in the second edition of his *Siècle de Louis XIV* (1751), one passage of which reads as follows: "Enfin, le siècle passé a mis celui où nous sommes en état de rassembler en un corps et de transmettre à la postérité le dépôt de toutes les sciences et de tous les arts, tous poussés aussi loin que l'industrie humaine a pu aller; et c'est à quoi a travaillé une société de savants remplis d'esprit et de lumières. Cet ouvrage immense et immortel semble accuser la brièveté des hommes." Moland, XIV, 153.

[17] Influenced by the Encyclopedists, the abbé de Prades wrote a thesis in theology for the Sorbonne in which he posited a sensualist interpretation of the soul. Forced to flee, the abbé found refuge at Potsdam, thanks to a request by Voltaire to Frederick. The incident had exposed the Encyclopedia to attacks from pious factions in France.

[18] Koser-Droysen, p. 377n3.

[19] "Il couchait au-dessous [de l'] appartement [du roi de Prusse]...Le roi composait en haut des ouvrages de philosophie, d'histoire, et de poésie; et son favori cultivait en bas les mêmes arts et les mêmes talents." Voltaire, *Commentaire historique sur les oeuvres de l'auteur de la Henriade*, Moland, 1, 93. Voltaire was speaking of himself in the third person.

acknowledged the receipt of Voltaire's first article [20]: "J'ai lu votre premier article, qui est très bon. Vous aurez commencé la table alphabétique des articles; je crois qu'il faudrait l'achever avant de commencer l'ouvrage." He then made further suggestions about the organization of the "dictionnaire" (Best. 4427), a preoccupation that reflects his administrative bent. In Best. 4428 Voltaire ridiculed an unnamed theological treatise in four volumes which Frederick had given him and offered His Majesty another sample of his work on the dictionary: "En qualité de Théologien de Belzebut oserai-je interrompre encor vos travaux par un petit mot d'édification sur l'athéisme que je mets à vos pieds? J'ay choisi ce petit morceau parmy les autres comme un des plus ortodoxes... si [Votre Majesté] daignait me corriger, je croirais alors l'ouvrage digne d'elle." He had completed several articles of which "Athéisme" was the most shocking and therefore the most likely to appeal to Frederick, whose criticism he invited. His references to devils and their works would become a standing joke in his correspondence concerning the dictionary. Frederick replied in Best. 4429: "Cet article me paraît très beau; il n'y a que le pari que je vous conseillerais de changer, à cause que vous vous êtes moqué de Pascal, qui se sert de la même figure. Remarquez encore, s'il vous plaît, que vous citez Epicure, Protagoras & c. qui vivraient dans la même ville; je crois qu'il ne faudrait pas citer des gens de lettres pour vivre tranquilles ensemble" [21]. However, an "Athée" containing allusions to Epicurus, Protagoras and a Pascalian bet did not appear in Voltaire's alphabetical works until the Kehl edition ("Athée" I), a fate which may have befallen other articles written at Potsdam.

In Best. 4430, most of which is in verse, Voltaire presented "Baptême" to Frederick, who acknowledged both this article and "Ame" in Best. 4431: "Si vous continuez du train dont vous allez, le dictionnaire sera fait en peu de temps. L'article de l'âme que je reçois, est bien fait; celui du *baptême* y est supérieur. Il semble que le hasard

---

[20] Koser and Droysen, who place Best. 4428 immediately before Best. 4427, claim that this article is "Athéisme", but Besterman says that the letter accompanying the unnamed article has been lost. One wonders if Voltaire also sent his first article to Wilhelmine on October 24: "Je prends la liberté de luy envoyer [à Votre altesse Roiale] un petit ouvrage de dévotion que j'ay fait pour mon très réverendissime père en Dieu le philosofe de Sans Souci". (Best. 3321) The "piety" of the work and the "prelacy" of Frederick remind one of the dictionary.

[21] Clifford Crist points out that the last part of this quotation was a premonition. Frederick went on in his letter to cite as an example the König-Maupertius quarrel which would soon set him and Voltaire against one another.

vous fait dire ce qui pourtant est la suite d'une méditation." Though soon disproved, the first sentence contributes to the general impression in these letters that Voltaire's production was remarkable after only a month of work. With Best. 4432 he sent Frederick "Abraham", a title mentioned by Collini. "Si V. M. jette les yeux sur cet article dans Bayle, elle verra que cette ébauche est plus pleine, plus curieuse et plus courte. Ce livre, honoré de quelques articles de votre main, ferait du bien au monde. Chérisac coulerait à fond les s^{ts} pères." The rivalry with Bayle supports Pomeau's contention that the urge to improve upon the cumbersome *Dictionnaire historique et critique* inspired Voltaire to create an encyclopedic work of his own. At this point he attributed his dictionary to one of the many imaginary authors of his works, Chérisac, whom he would later replace by Desbuttes. His invitation to Frederick implies that he would have gladly directed a project in which the king of Prussia would be a mere collaborator. One wonders how Frederick reacted to this proposal.

But Voltaire did not stop there. Instead he devoted the rest of his letter to a lengthy apology for and of a "mémoire détaillé" which he had sent Frederick. The unusual prolixity of this passage as well as its awkward mixture of self-condemnation and supplication betray the embarrassed courtier who knew he was imposing on the generosity of his prince: "Il y aurait une prodigieuse indiscrétion à moy de pro-poser de nouvelles dépenses à V. M. pour mes fantaisies, quand elle me donne 5000 écus par an pour ne rien faire" (Best. 4432). His fear of having irritated the parsimonious Frederick scarcely veiled his rash hopes. The quotation shows that the word *mémoire* means an actual estimate of the expenses necessary for the execution of the dictionary project [22]. Other details emerge in the following paragraph:

> Je ne connais que le stile des personnes que j'ay voulu attirer icy pour travailler, et point leur caractère. Il se pourrait qu'étant em-ployées par V. M. à un ouvrage qui ne laisse pas d'être délicat et qui demande le secret, elles fissent les difficiles, s'en allassent, et vous compromissent. En me chargeant de tout sous vos ordres, V. M. n'était compromise en rien. (Best. 4432)

In response to Frederick's suggestion that he draw up a table of con-tents, Voltaire seems to have proposed something far more ambitious. His list of articles apparently included the names of the collaborators

---

[22] "Voltaire scheint ... einen genauen Plan des Dictionnaire mit Liste der Mit-arbeiter und eine Berechnung des Kosten dem Könige vorgelegt zu haben." Koser-Droysen, p. 382n1.

who would write them and the pensions His Majesty would have to pay if they came to Potsdam to work under Voltaire's direction. It is a shame that this *mémoire* has been lost. Was he asking to invite Diderot, d'Alembert and their collaborators on the *Encyclopédie* to join him in exile? In any case, his own encyclopedia would be a more serious offensive against "superstition" than they could possibly hope to mount in Paris. Whatever form it took, Frederick's answer was certainly negative. Voltaire had already demonstrated his determination to create the work, with or without a royal subsidy.

More generous with his criticism, the king commented on the article "Julien le philosophe" in Best. 4447, which probably belonged to the same series of letters between him and his "writer-in-residence": "Il pourra devenir excellent, si vous y ajoutez les raisons pour & contre sa conversion." Julian was a Roman emperor who abjured Christianity. It is unfortunate that Voltaire did not heed Frederick's advice, for "Julien", which he would insert in the *Portatif* only in 1767, is disappointing for this very reason. He did not mention Frederick's criticism in his reply (Best. 4445), with which he sent "Moïse", and their correspondence over the dictionary terminated with this letter. In "Moïse" Voltaire used chronological evidence to cast doubt on Moses' authorship of the *Pentateuch*: "Plusieurs savants ont cru que le *Pentateuque* ne peut avoir été écrit par Moïse. Ils disent que par l'Ecriture même il est avéré que le premier exemplaire connu fut trouvé du temps du roi Josias" (pp. 320—321). He was making the same point, a commonplace at the time [23], in his *Défense de milord Bolingbroke* (published 20 November 1752), in which he defended deism from Samuel Formey of the Berlin Academy. On November 4 he wrote Formey as follows: "Le roi ... se moque des disputes théologiques ... Laissez les profanes douter de la chronologie de Moïse" (Best. 4435). Only the uninitiated would merely doubt anything so obviously false. Voltaire's preoccupation with this subject, also apparent in his notebooks, seems to have caused him to deviate from his production of dictionary articles by alphabetical order which had apparently gone no further than the letter B. A special interest in Julian may have also led him to write this article ahead of time.

His mention of the king in the letter to Formey above implies that he was still on good terms with Frederick in early November. His support of König in the quarrel with Maupertuis, who as president

---

[23] "Whether Esdras or Moses had been responsible for the redaction of the *Pentateuch* was a raging theological controversy in the eighteenth century." Ages, "Voltaire and Thieriot", *Dalhousie Review*, XLVII, 45n5.

of the Berlin Academy had the king's support, would soon erupt in the *Akakia* scandal [24]. But this crisis did not prevent Voltaire from sending a dictionary article to the marquis d'Argens, a colleague in the Academy: "Je vous prie de lire attentivement l'art. ci-joint du Dictionnaire de *scriberius audens, et de me le rendre, et de m'en dire votre avis. Je suis fâché que vous ne vous appliquez plus à ces baga-telles rabbiniques, théologiques et diaboliques*" [25] (Best. 4462). By December 18, however, Voltaire was only interested in a dictionary that would expose Frederick's doubletalk: "*Mon ami* signifie *mon esclave . . . Souper avec moi ce soir,* signifie *je me moquerai de vous ce soir*" (Best. 4486). This letter to his niece and mistress Mme. Denis marked the beginning of a seven-year period during which he neg-lected the dictionary for limited collaboration on the Encyclopedia. In March of 1753, moreover, he left Prussia for good. But he had already completed a significant number of articles in only a few months and apparently even composed a table of contents. Although he appears to have heeded Frederick's advice only on this point, the interest of the "enlightened monarch" obviously spurred his efforts. One is tempted to speculate on how soon he would have been able to publish the work, what form it would have taken and the effect it would have had if he had been able to finish it at Potsdam.

The brief but concentrated experience he had acquired in planning a "philosophical dictionary" and writing articles for it apparently intensified his interest in the Encyclopedia. From Colmar on 21 May 1754 he sent Mme. Denis his dictionary article "Ame" as a sample of his encyclopedic work, inviting her to show it to Diderot and d'Alembert. In another letter written at about the same time he told d'Alembert of this article and included two others, "Eloquence" and "Elégance", which d'Alembert had requested for the *Encyclopédie*. His attitude towards this collaboration is surprisingly humble: "Si vous croyez devoir faire entrer ces rocailles dans votre grand temple, il n'y a point à Paris d'aide à maçon qui n'en sache plus que moi, et qui ne vous serve mieux. D'ailleurs, ne suffit il pas, dans un diction-naire, de définir, d'expliquer, de donner quelques exemples? faut il discuter les ouvrages de tous ceux qui ont écrit sur la matière dont on parle?" (Best. 5173). *Définir, expliquer, donner quelques exemples*: This formula, which applies to the *Portatif*, is more flexible than it appears at first glance. It not only permits the encyclopedist to

---

[24] Voltaire's *Diatribe du docteur Akakia* is a satire of Maupertuis' behavior during the quarrel. The scandal was due to the publication of this work and Fre-derick's attempts to intimidate its author.

[25] D'Argens was the author of the *Lettres juives* (1738).

satisfy the curiosity of most readers without boring them, but also to reduce to rational terms any mystery that may be essential to the phenomenon being defined, explained and exemplified, in particular, sacred mystery.

He no doubt applied this critical method during the several weeks he spent that summer at the Benedictine Abbey of Senones. A guest of Dom Calmet, whom he would later betray in the *Portatif*, he gave himself to study of the Bible, exploiting the resources of his friend's library. The materials he accumulated during this visit probably facilitated the compostion of many a dictionary article in later years.

Continuing his discussions of encyclopedic technique with d'Alembert, he furnished the Encyclopedia with forty-three articles over the next few years, only two of which would also appear in the *Portatif*: "Messie" and "Idole, Idolâtre, Idolâtrie". In the latter he discreetly but convincingly presented historical evidence to show that pagans did not worship images any more than Christians, but rather the deity represented. It was on 28 December 1756 that, out of probable impatience with the benign articles he had been assigned [26], he asked d'Alembert for permission to contribute such an essay to the Encyclopedia:

> Avez vous *Idole* et *Idolâtre?* ... Jamais on n'a adoré les idoles; jamais culte public n'a été institué pour du bois et de la pierre: le peuple les a traitées comme il traite nos saints. Le sujet est délicat, mais il comporte de bien bonnes vérités qu'on peut dire. (Best. 6403)

There is no record of d'Alembert's reply, but it must have been affirmative since Voltaire sent the completed article with a letter to him on 4 February 1757.

By this time, however, the scandal over the article "Genève" and the *cacouac* affair had driven d'Alembert from his co-editorship [27].

---

[26] [Les entrepreneurs de l'*Encyclopédie*] me donnent quelquefois des articles peu intéressants à faire," he wrote Thieriot on 5 January 1758. (Best. 6860).

[27] "Genève," which appeared in volume VII of the *Encyclopédie* (1757), was authored by d'Alembert, but heavily influenced and perhaps edited by Voltaire. Though laudatory, it met with a storm of protest from Genevan pastors and authorities. The *Nouveau mémoire pour servir à l'histoire des Cacouacs* (1757) by Jacob Moreau was part of a propaganda campaign against the Encyclopedists or *cacouacs*, monsters who enjoyed doing evil. Disgusted and outraged, d'Alembert resigned a position that exposed him to such attacks. He may have felt "qu'il se faut prester à autruy et ne se donner qu'à soy-mesme." Montaigne, "De mesnager sa Volonté," in *Essais* (Paris, 1950), p. 1124.

Voltaire eventually took his side against Diderot and demanded the return of the articles he had contributed to the Encyclopedia. Angered by Diderot's failure to answer, he apparently wrote him a letter, which has since been lost, naming the articles. On February 13 he told d'Alembert: "J'ay encor écrit pour que Diderot me renvoye mes lettres, [mes articles et] idolâtrie ... Je ne veux pas doresnavant fournir une ligne à l'enciclopédie" (Best. 6936). Diderot finally answered, two days later, informing him that d'Alembert had his articles. This letter led to a reconciliation and brief renewal of collaboration by d'Alembert and Volaire. On May 19 Voltaire actually complained to the comte d'Argental because Diderot had not yet agreed to take his articles back: "J'ay fait des recherches très pénibles pour rendre les articles histoire et idolâtrie intéressants et instructifs ... Je vous demande en grâce d'exiger de Diderot une réponse catégorique et prompte" (Best. 7040). Finally on June 14 Diderot sent him an obliviously gracious letter purporting to accept anything he had written for the Encyclopedia.

Voltaire must have received advance word of his consent, for just two days later he told d'Argental that he was forwarding "Idole" and "Imagination". He adds:

> C'est une entreprise hardie de prouver qu'il n'y a point eu d'idolâtres. Je crois la chose prouvée et je crains de l'avoir trop démontrée. C'est à vous à protéger les véritez délicates que j'ay dittes dans les articles *idolâtrie* et *imagination*. Elles pouront passer au tribunal des examinateurs si elles ne sont pas annoncées sous mon nom. Ce nom est dangereux, et met tout bon téologien en garde [28].   (Best. 7060)

The name was dangerous because the writer was known to have published far more provocative texts than the usual Encyclopedia fare. Anonymity for "Idole" would hopefully permit this militant article to lose itself among the more innocent ones like "Imagination". This attempt to "penetrate" the Encyclopedia does not appear to have fooled Diderot, since "Idole" is one of merely two "philosophical" articles (the other is "Histoire") which, after some hesitation, he accepted from Voltaire. By situation and temperament the two writers were as different from each other as the alphabetical works they produced.

The delay in having "Idole" accepted must have suggested to Voltaire that Diderot would take militant articles more readily if

---

[28] Voltaire seems to be referring to the Faculté de Théologie of the University of Paris, who in principle had the right to censure a work after publication. In practice, these "good theologians" had lost most of this power to Parlament by 1756.

they appeared to have been written by a more obscure "philosopher". He therefore recruited the calvinist minister Polier de Bottens who had furnished him with etymological data for his part of the Encyclopedia article "Fornication" (d'Alembert wrote the other part). Feigning a preoccupation with other matters, he gleefully inspired, edited and submitted seventeen articles by Polier, all of which found their way into the *Encyclopédie*. "[Ces articles] procèdent d'une intention évidente", says Naves: "c'est de discréditer les controverses théologiques et les récits fabuleux de la Bible, dont un chrétien raisonnable et civilisé du XVIIIe siècle ne peut rien tirer de satisfaisant" [29]. Since this strategy coincides with that of Voltaire in his dictionary project, one can only conclude that he had succeeded in slipping his kind of "philosophy" into the Encyclopedia. Polier's most daring essay was "Messie", the only other one (with "Idole") to appear in both the *Encyclopédie* and the *Portatif*. "Je lui ai donné *Messie* à faire", Voltaire told d'Alembert on 29 August 1757, "nous verrons comme il s'en tirera" (Best. 6663). Naves says that Polier was writing it in October, but the title disappeared from Voltaire's correspondence until 1764 when he published it in the *Portatif*. Both "Messie" and "Idole" would appear in the *Encyclopédie* itself only a year later.

Yet these articles probably would have appeared in the Encyclopedia alone, if Voltaire's old dream of bringing the project under his influence in a foreign country had come true [30]. Having made one attempt in Potsdam, he tried again in Lausanne during the crisis of d'Alembert's resignation, which threatened to stop the *Encyclopédie* at volume VII. Early in January 1758 he told d'Alembert (Best.6865) and implied in a letter to Diderot (Best. 6862) that the work on the Encyclopedia should have been done "dans un pays libre" (Best. 6865). But he was more specific in a letter dated February 26, which he asked the comte d'Argental to show Diderot:

> Cette entreprise immense vaudra donc à mᵣ Diderot environ trente mille livres! Elle devrait luy en valoir deux cent mille (j'entends à luy et à mᵣ Dalembert et à une ou deux personnes qui les secondent),

---

[29] *Voltaire et l'Encyclopédie*, p. 141.

[30] He had manifested his desire to found a colony of men of letters in a letter to Cideville in 1740: "Quand vivrons nous ensemble? car vous savez bien que nous ... vivrons [à Rouen]. Il faut qu'à la fin le petit nombre des adeptes se rassemble dans un petit coin de terre. Nous y serons comme les bons israelites en AEgypte qui avoient la lumière pour eux tout seules à ce qu'on dit, pendant que la cour de Pharaon étoit dans les ténèbres." (Best. 2021).

et s'ils avaient voulu seulement honorer le petit trou de Lausane de leurs travaux, je leur aurais fait mon billet de deux cent mille livres.
(Best. 6956)

Thus Voltaire now had enough confidence in his wealth and business acumen to offer on his own what he had earlier felt obligated to ask of Frederick. He may have even based this proposal, which seems generous, on the estimate he had drawn up in Potsdam. On March 7 he repeated the offer to d'Alembert, insisting that it was still open: "Peutêtre si on s'entendait, si on avait du courage, si on osait prendre une résolution on pourait très bien ... imprimer ici [l'enciclopédie]" (Best. 6970). On both occasions, moreover, his language suggests that he had already proposed to bring the Encyclopedia to Lausanne, his winter residence during the past few years, on an earlier occasion, perhaps d'Alembert's visit in August 1756. It would be a mistake of course to take this generosity at face value, because financial control by such a strong-willed Maecenas would probably lead to something like total control. At best, Voltaire was seeking to promote his kind of "philosophy"; at worst, he was trying to appropriate the Encyclopedia. Despite the situation in Paris, neither d'Alembert nor Diderot apparently ever bothered to reply to his proposal.

This situation took a turn for the worse on 6 February 1759 when Parlement condemned the *Encyclopédie* along with Helvétius' *Esprit* (1758), which had created a convenient scandal, and on March 8 the government rekoved Diderot's "privilege" to publish the great work. Voltaire reacted with anger against the persecution, regrets for his fellow collaborators and the determination to compose his own encyclopedia [31]. The two great weaknesses he saw in the Encyclopedia had now proved irremediable: it would neither escape the stiffling censorship of its self-righteous enemies, nor attain the militant concision he deemed necessary for a "philosophical" dictionary. Early in 1759 he appended a long note (entitled, in 1771, "Note de Morza") to his ode commemorating the death of Frederick's sister the margravine of Bayreuth, in which he not only satirized the foes of the Encyclopedia, but also made a familiar criticism of the Encyclopedia itself: "Beaucoup de nos méchants confrères ont manqué à la principale règle d'un dictionnaire, qui est de se contenter d'une définition

---

[31] "Il n'est pas exagéré d'avancer," Naves concludes, "que cette *aventure* [celle de l'*Encyclopédie*] est à l'origine du *Dictionnaire philosophique*, beaucoup plus que le fameux souper du roi de Prusse." *Voltaire et l'Encyclopédie*, p. 65. Naves ignores the evidence that much of the dictionary already existed in manuscript form from the Prussian sojourn.

courte et juste, d'un précepte clair et juste, et de deux ou trois exemples utiles" (Moland, VIII, 477). Although he intended this note as a statement of solidarity with the encyclopedists, he would soon terminate his collaboration on the project.

"Ce n'était pas en France qu'il fallait faire cet ouvrage" (Best. 7567), he reminded d'Alembert on May 4. But the latter's ex-colleague Diderot had not forgotten Voltaire's offer to bring the Encyclopedia to Lausanne. He entrusted his friend Grimm, who was visiting his mistress Mme. d'Epinay in Geneva that summer, with a proposal for the old man, whose prestige and collaboration the *Encyclopédie* now sorely needed. "Dites-lui, pour le mettre à son aise", he instructed Grimm on August 18, ". . . que tout paroîtra à la fois, soit ici avec permission tacite, soit en Hollande, soit à Genève où j'irai" [32]. If Grimm transmitted this message as accurately as one might have expected of him, Voltaire could not have failed to understand that Diderot was offering him a compromise: If the latter could not obtain "tacite permission" [33] to publish in France, he would go into exile to accomplish the task according to Voltaire's long-standing desire. But the phrase "pour le mettre à son aise" implies that Diderot did not intend to resort to such a move and Voltaire, who may have detected this hypocrisy, refused to resume collaboration on the Encyclopedia.

He did not abandon the idea of moving the project to a more favorable location in his vicinity. On 7 January 1760 he renewed the proposition in a letter to Mme. d'Epinay: "On m'assure que Diderot est devenu riche: si celà est, qu'il envoye promener les libraires, les persécuteurs et les sots, et qu'il vienne vivre en homme libre entre Gex et Genève" (Best. 7971). Supposing this "feeler" came to Diderot's attention, one wonders if he noticed the irony of "freedom" between Gex and Geneva, with the meddlesome Voltaire and the suspicious parsons as neighbors. In any case Diderot did not answer.

In the same letter to Mme. d'Epinay Voltaire also discussed the problems involved in composing an article "Idée" for the *Encyclopédie*. He had asked d'Alembert for permission to write such an

---

[32] *Correspondance*, ed. Georges Roth, II, 173.

[33] "Quand on distigue qu'un livre n'est pas conforme en tout point à la doctrine de l'autorité, on préfère, puisqu'il faut lui donner une permission, ne pas la reconnaître officiellement et délivrer une Permission Tacite." Robert Estivals, *la Statistique Bibliographique de la France . . . au XVIIIe siècle* (Paris, 1965), p. 43.

article in 1756 [34] and met with a refusal. "Comment traiter *idée?*" he nevertheless asked Mme. d'Epinay. "Ma levrette coucha ces jours passées, et je vis clairement qu'elle avait des *idées* ... Les idées sont une modification de la matière, et nous ne sçavons point ce que c'est que cette matière, et nous n'en connaissons que quelques propriétés" (Best. 7971). He expressed the same sort of scepticism in his own dictionary article "Idée" (1765): "Qu'est-ce qu'une idée?" (p. 235). But he followed a different line of reasoning in this text. Instead of studying idea as a modification of matter, he considered it an image formed in the mind [35]. Since the latter concept seems superior to the former, it is possible that his thinking progressed from one to the other. It appears unlikely that he would have brought the subject up, unless he were working on such an article at the time.

Even more convincing evidence of a return to his own dictionary project occurs in a letter to Mme. du Deffand on 18 February 1760. As an excuse for not having written more often, he told her: "Je suis absorbé dans un compte que je me rends à moi-même par ordre alphabétique, de tout ce que je dois penser de ce monde cy et sur l'autre, le tout, pour mon usage, et peut-être après ma mort, pour l'usage des honnêtes gens" (Best. 8028). Having compared himself then to Montaigne, he supposed that some of the articles in this "dictionnaire d'idées" would amuse his blind correspondent. While the identity of the work is clear, its purpose seems to have changed, for in 1752 he obviously thought of the dictionary as a public attack on religious authority. In the letter to Mme. du Deffand above he said that the work would be for himself rather than the public, or at least until after his death. The second version is suspect, however, and even more suspect the reference to Montaigne. Meditation in the manner of the great essayist scarcely harmonizes with Voltaire's nervous energy and in 1760 he was as busy spreading his "philosophical" gospel as ever. Certainly the account he proposed to "render unto himself" was really meant for the "gentle folk" of his reading public whom he seldom kept waiting, least of all until after his

---

[34] "Vous ou m. Diderot, vous ferez sans doute *Idée* et *Imagination;* si vous n'y travaillez pas, et que la place soit vacante, je suis à vos ordres." (Best. 6375).

[35] According to the prevalent view, shared by Descartes and Locke, an idea was an image in the mind. Idea as a modification of matter appears to be a simplification of Spinoza's *Ethics:* "The actual intellect whether finite or infinite, must comprehend the attributes of God and the modifications of God and nothing else." ([New York, 1949], p. 66). Like many of his contemporaries, Voltaire probably interpreted Spinoza's *substance* (God or Nature) as *matter,* hence the belief that Spinoza was a materialist.

death [36]. Letters to Mme. du Deffand had to be read aloud and her visitors were not necessarily discreet or friendly to Voltaire [37]. The concept of an alphabetical self-guide was probably a subterfuge to inform friends and confuse enemies. It may also have been a crafty anticipation of future denials that he had authored the *Portatif*.

In addition to "Idée", his correspondence in 1760 contains less specific allusions to other articles that would appear in this work, such as "Salomon". In a letter on April 15 to count Lorenzi, a fellow member of the Società Botanica Fiorentina, he regretted the disappearance of a treatise on plants "depuis le cèdre jusqu'à l'hysope" [38] attributed to the Old Testament king. "C'était sans doute un très bel ouvrage", he says, "puisqu'il était composé par un roi". (Best. 8118) This irony does not hide his curiosity about what may have been an ancient version of the "enlightened monarch", an encyclopedist [39] or a "philosopher" like the king of Prussia, whom, when the latter behaved, he was fond of calling the "Salomon du Nord". Although Voltaire failed to mention Solomon's alleged work on plants in the *Portatif*, he made much the same remark about all of his books: "Les livres attribués à Salomon ont duré plus que son temple. C'est peut-être une des grandes preuves de la force des préjugés et de la faiblesse de l'esprit humain ... On les a crus bons parce

---

[36] He made the same claim for volume III of his *Essai sur l'histoire générale* (later entitled *Essai sur les moeurs*) in his preface to the 1754 Walther edition: "Il est vrai que dans ce volume que je donne malgré moi, je laisse toujours voir l'effet qu'ont fait sur mon esprit les objets que je considère. Mais ce compte que je rendais de mes lectures avec une naïveté qu'on n'a presque jamais quand on écrit pour le public, est précisément ce qui pourra être utile." (Paris, 1963), p. 888. The claim is as questionable for this work as for the *Portatif*.

[37] The following speaks for itself: "Ah! J'oubliois de vous dire que je suis furieuse de ce qui vient d'arriver. On a imprimé sans mon consentement à mon insçu la lettre [Best. 10829] que vous m'avez Ecritte avant la dernière." (Best. 10933 from Mme. du Deffand to Voltaire on 14 March 1764).

[38] Voltaire is quoting from I *Kings* 4:33 in the *Bible*. The same passage had inspired the following verses in his *Défense du Mondain* (1737): "C'est Salomon, ce sage fortuné, / Roi philosophe, et Platon couronné, / Qui connut tout, du cèdre jusqu'à l'herbe: / Vit-on jamais un luxe plus superbe?" Moland, X, 93.

[39] "It was [God] who gave me [Solomon] true knowledge of all that is, who taught me the structure of the world and the properties of the elements, the beginning, end and middle of the times, the alternation of the solstices and the succession of the seasons, the revolution of the year and the positions of the stars, the natures of animals and the instincts of wild beasts, the powers of spirits and the mental processes of men, the varieties of plants and the medical properties of roots." *The Book of Wisdom* 7:17—20 in *The Jerusalem Bible* (New York, 1966).

qu'on les a crus d'un roi, et que ce roi passait pour le plus sage des hommes (p. 379). While *parce que* replaces *puisque* here, both of these conjuctions link dependent to independent clauses in the same ironical way [40], which conveys Voltaire's resentment of Frederick. In the letter he used many fewer words to express the same idea, for he could expect greater subtlety from Lorenzi than his general public.

Assuming in the letter that a knowledge of herbs produced the usual competence in medecine, he joked: "[Salomon] était apparemment le premier médecin de ses sept cents femmes et de ses trois cents concubines". (Best. 8118) That Salomon should prefer wives to concubines intrigued Voltaire, who brought the subject up again in "Salomon": "On lui ... donne sept cents [femmes] qui portent le nom de *reines;* et ce qui est étrange, c'est qu'il n'avait que trois cents concubines" (p. 378). Common sense, to which Voltaire was appealing here, indicated that concubines would be more convenient in such numbers than wives [41], a fact that exposed the awesome Solomon to ridicule. Again, a rapid allusion in his letter became a careful explanation in the *Portatif.*

His research on religious questions necessitated the procurement of works like William Warburton's *Divine Legation of Moses Demonstrated,* Books 1—3 (1738) of which George Keate had sent him in 1757. On 15 April 1760 he admired this author in a letter to Keate. "Mais je n'ai que [les] deux premiers tomes de la légation de Moÿse", he hints; "je ne sçais comment m'y prendre pour avoir les deux derniers volumes" (Best. 8120). But Keate did not take the hint to supply him with Books 4—6 (1741), and so he pestered his lazy friend Thieriot for them in four letters written during June and July. Finally he acknowledged receipt of the remaining text on August 11: "Ouy, j'ay mon Moyse complet. Il a fait le pentateuque comme vous et moy" (Best. 8379) [42]. As we have seen, his scepticism about Moses'

---

[40] "On rencontre ... [dans le *Dictionnaire philosophique*] des phrases où c'est la conjonction de subordination qui devient ironique lorsqu'elle unit deux propositions n'ayant aucun rapport logique." Jeanne Monty, *Etude sur le style polémique de Voltaire: le Dictionnaire philosophique* in *SVEC,* XLIV.

[41] "Je ne prétends pas autoriser la pluralité des femmes, à Dieu ne plaise! Je crois qu'une seule suffit à la fois, pour le bonheur d'un galant homme." Voltaire, *Lettre civile et honnête* (1760), Moland XXIV, 147.

[42] Best. 8794 (21 Jan. 1761) and Best. 8403 (undated) also informed Thieriot that the missing volumes had arrived. Had Thieriot failed to receive the earlier letters or sent extra copies? There are two editions of the work in the catalogue of the Ferney library.

autorship of the *Pentateuch* had inspired the article "Moïse" in 1752 [43].

His interest in *Moses' Legation* was motivated at least in part by Warburton's demonstration that "les [anciens] Juifs n'attendaient point une autre vie" (Best 8120). Voltaire borrowed this argument [44] to undermine the Old Testament foundation of Christianity in "Ame" and "Athée", versions of which he had shown Frederick in Potsdam, in "Enfer" which he actually derived from the Englishman's work [45], and in the "Première Question" of the article "Religion", which begins with a paragraph in loose translation from Book 1, Section 1 of the same source: "Le judaïsme n'est pas fondé sur la créance d'une autre vie, donc le judaïsme a été soutenu par une providence extraordinaire" (p. 359). Voltaire turned this proposition against its author, a defender of the Anglican faith, to show that it did not strengthen his apology, but rather weakened it. In "Enfer" Voltaire mentioned neither Warburton nor Moses in condemning the assumption by eighteenth-century theologians that the ancient Hebrews had believed in the possibility of punishment for their transgressions in a life after death: "Il est ridicule de croire, ou de feindre de croire, sur quelques passages très obscurs, que l'enfer était admis par les anciennes lois des juifs ... quand l'auteur de ces lois ne dit pas un seul mot qui puisse avoir le moindre rapport avec les châtiments de la vie future" (p. 178). Warburton devoted Book 6 of the *Legation* to proof that, according to Scripture, they had no idea either of punishment or reward in an afterlife. But this book is in volume IV of the 1755 edition and volume III of the 1738—1742 edition, both of which appear in the catalogue of the Ferney library [46]. One cannot say to which of these editions Voltaire was referring in his letter to Keate, but he obviously did not have the text of the sixth and final book at the time. He

---

[43] Another book sought by Voltaire that year was the *Observations sur un livre intitulé De l'Esprit des Lois* (1753) by Claude Dupin. Voltaire asked Mme. Dupin for a copy on May 22. He may have been working on Section I of "Lois (Des)" in which he gave some of his own opinions on Montesquieu's subject.

[44] Warburton's intentions were entirely different: "My declared purpose in this work is to demonstrate *the divine legation* of Moses, in order to use it for the foundation of a projected defence of Revelation in general, as the Dispensation [of Moses] is completed in Christianity." *The Divine Legation of Moses Demonstrated* (London, 1811), V, 294.

[45] On this point Pomeau confirms Clifford Crist who confirms Voltaire himself in Best. 11320, except that the latter did not admit his authorship of the article.

[46] See George Havens and Norman Torrey, *Voltaire's Catalogue of his Library at Ferney* in SVEC IX.

adapted the complete thesis of this book to "Ame": "Moïse en aucun endroit ne propose aux Juifs des récompenses et des peines dans une autre vie ... il ne leur parle jamais de l'immortalité de leurs âmes" (p. 11). The necessity for belief in punishment and reward also prompted Voltaire to include in "Athée" a passage echoing the ancient Hebrew ignorance of the immortal soul: "Les lois de Moïse ... n'enseignent point de châtiments après la mort, n'enseignent point aux premiers Juifs l'immortalité de l'âme" (p. 40). Thus opposing Bayle's contention that a community of atheists would live together no less harmoniously than any other, Voltaire claimed that the fear of divine justice in this life sufficed to regulate Hebrew society.

His preoccupation with punishment and reward in "Athée", which in the *Portatif* replaced the "Athéisme" he had shown Frederick in 1752, suggests that he wrote it after 11 August 1760. Although "Enfer" treats of punishment alone, the same may be said for it. But Voltaire may have written the "Première Question" of "Religion" before this date, since he organized it around a translated passage from Book 1 of the *Legation*. He must have inserted the statement of Warburton's thesis in "Ame", already composed in Potsdam, sometime in 1760, but he could have drawn it either from Book 1, where the author of the *Legation* summarized it in advance, or Book 6, where he actually developped it. In any event, the available information does not guarantee this attempt to establish the chronology of the four articles.

On April 25 of the same year Voltaire playfully compared his *belle philosophe* Mme. d'Epinay to Confucius, whose humanitarian philosophy [47] he admired. His enthuisiasm for the Chinese philosopher may have been contemporaneous with his composition of the "Catéchisme chinois", which followed the article "Chine" in the early editions of the *Portatif*. This dialogue in six *entretiens* between a young prince and his governor, a disciple of Confucius, is a moral lesson based on Voltaire's "philosophical" interpretation of Confucius' teaching.

His publisher Gabriel Cramer offered further indications of work on the dictionary in a letter to Grimm in May. Obviously pleased with Voltaire's production, he listed the works he expected to print. „Nous avons sur le métier", he added, "un certain dictionnaire dont

---

[47] Besterman dates the letter, from which the following passage was taken, as ca. 1760: "Les ressorts de sagesse que Confucius imagina, il y a plus de deux mille ans, ont encore leur effet à la Chine." (Best. 8275 from Voltaire to Jean François Bastide). This additional evidence suggests that his interest in Confucius at the time was not just passing fancy.

nous parlerons, & qui fera du bruit; c'est un ouvrage commencé il y a 20 ans & dont personne n'a jamais rien vû" (Best. 8172). Even though the work was only eight years old and not as secret as Cramer says, his expectations show that Voltaire had been talking about it and probably writing articles for it. Since Cramer predicted that it would attract attention, one may assume that Voltaire had shown him some of the articles.

It was in 1760 that the latter acquired another friend, who would serve him well during the composition and publication of the *Portatif*. The chief clerk of the *vingtième* office, or Old Regime equivalent of the Internal Revenue Service, was Etienne Damilaville, a dedicated "philosopher" and devoted friend of Diderot. "Il avait le droit par sa place", explains Gustave Desnoireterres, "de contresigner, avec le cachet du contrôleur général des finances, toutes les lettres sortant de son bureau, et il usait largement de ce privilège en faveur de ses amis, auxquels il faisait ainsi passer, d'un bout à l'autre du royaume, tous les paquets, gros ou petits, qu'ils pouvaient souhaiter" [48]. To Voltaire, whose correspondence with Paris was both risky and vital, such a service had great appeal. Consequently we find him cultivating Damilaville on September 3: "Si vos occupations vous permettaient de me dire quelquefois des nouvelles de la littérature, et surtout de m. Diderot, ce serait une nouvelle obligation que je vous aurais" (Best. 8433). Thus Voltaire renewed his contact with the Encyclopedia which had been ruptured by d'Alembert's resignation. But Damilaville would prove even more helpful in running errands, conducting business and transmitting information, especially in connection with the *Portatif*.

Further apparent allusions to articles for this work appear in Voltaire's correspondence during the winter of 1760—1761, and several of them reveal an interest in the fourth-century Arian schism. The Alexandrian priest Arius insisted on the subordination of Christ to God, while his enemies, Athanasius bishop of Alexandria among them, contended that the Son's deity equaled the Father's. This dispute, which caused long and widespread strife, served Voltaire's purpose in the *Portatif* of undermining the authority of the Catholic Church. Among other references to this controversy [49], he asked the

---

[48] *Voltaire et la société du XVIIIe siècle*, V, (Paris, 1875), p. 243.

[49] In Best. 8078 (24 March 1760) and Best. 8792 (20 Jan. 1761). In the latter, he also said: "[Le] Roy de Prusse ... parle des Chrétiens comme Julien en parlait." He had written "Julien le philosophe" in 1752 as we have seen, but the subject was a constant preoccupation with him.

Calvinist minister Jacob Vernes in November: "Que dites vous de cet ... évêque qui pria le bon dieu de faire mourir Arius lors qu'il allait à l'église, et qui fut exaucé?" (Best. 8621) [50]. In "Christianisme" he gave the circumstances of this curse which the Athanasian bishop Macarius placed on the head of Arius, who was on his way to a reconciliation with the other side. "Saint Macaire pria Dieu si ardemment de faire mourir Arius avant que ce prêtre pût entrer dans la Cathédrale", he stated, "que Dieu exauça sa prière" (p. 132). In the futility of the Arian schism and the mythical revenge of an orthodox god, which symbolized the hypocrisy of Christanity, Voltaire saw a shameful and therefore vulnerable chink in the moral armor of the Church. His interest in this question suggests that he was working on "Christianisme" at the time, and perhaps "Arius" as well.

Mme. du Deffand, who suffered from boredom, had asked for copies of such articles in her answer to Voltaire's letter announcing his "dictionnaire d'idées" earlier that year [51]. On December 9 he wrote that he was sending her two small manuscripts, one of which "est une plaisante découverte que j'ay faitte dans mon ami Ezéchiel" (Best 8683). Ezekiel, he said, was an "homme inimitable". To learn why, one must consult "Ezéchiel" in the *Portatif*, which was probably the manuscript in question. In this article Voltaire delighted in deciding what sort of excrement the Lord expected Ezekiel to eat with his bread [52]. "Comme il n'est point d'usage de manger de telles confitures

---

[50] He likewise sends Vernes "*un Pierre* [qui] n'est pas Simon Barjone," or a copy of his *Histoire de l'empire de Russie sous Pierre le grand*, volume I (1760), and not Jesus' disciple. The latter is the subject of "Pierre" in the *Portatif*. This pun appears in several of Voltaire's letters from the period.

[51] Here is the appropriate passage from Mme. du Deffand's letter: "Ce que vous appelez vos rogatons monsieur, m'ont fait un grand plaisir; vous devriez bien m'envoyer des articles du dictionnaire de vos idées, cela serait délicieux, et c'est cela qui me ferait penser." (Best. 8080).

[52] "Take this food in the shape of a barkley cake baked where they can see you, over human dung ... I will grant you cow's dung instead of human dung; you are to bake your bread on that ..." *Ezekiel* 4:12, 15, in *The Jerusalem Bible*. The editor notes: "Dried dung is used as fuel in the East". Voltaire, who probably did not have this information, seems to have borrowed his interpretation from Matthew Tindal's *Christianity as Old as Création* (1730). Le Maistre de Sacy's translation of the *Vulgate* (1730) may also have misled him: "Vous le couvrirez devant eux de l'ordure qui sort de l'homme" (12); "Vous ferez cuire votre pain sous cette fiente." (15) Robert Estienne's edition (1532) of the *Bible* presents: "Stercore quod egreditur de homine, operies illud in oculis eorū" (12); "Facies panem tuum in eo." (15) Evidently the sense of *operies* and *in eo* depends on the knowledge that dung was used as fuel. All three of the works mentioned were in the Ferney library. It would be unfair to accuse Voltaire of willfully misinterpreting *Ezekiel*.

sur son pain", he moralized, "la plupart des hommes trouvent ces commandements indignes de la majesté divine" (p. 191). On 15 January 1761 he answered a reply from Mme. du Deffand as follows: "Vous méprisez trop Ezéchiel, Madame... Je vous passe de ne déjeuner comme lui" (Best. 8772). He used the same kind of joke in "Ezéchiel", simply replacing the verb *déjeuner* by the equivalent noun: "A l'égard des raisons que Dieu pouvait avoir d'ordonner un tel déjeuner au prophète, ce n'est pas à nous de le demander" (p. 191). However, this benign acceptance of God's will was nothing more than an ironical pose typical of Voltaire in the *Portatif* [53]. His interest in Ezekiel's predicament arose from his fascination with the odd practices of ancient peoples and his comic taste for the obscene. He knew that neither Mme. du Deffand nor his public would blame him for transgressions against eighteenth-century propriety in the sacred text, which would be discredited in their eyes.

Ezekiel also provided him with a contradiction of Moses which further undermined the authority of the Old Testament. On January 15 he informed Mme. du Deffand that "[Ezéchiel] fut le premier qui osat donner un démenti à Moyse... il s'avisa d'assurer que Dieu ne punissait pas les enfans des iniquités de leurs pères" (Best. 8772). The Portatif echoes: "[Ezechiel] dit que le fils ne portera plus l'iniquité de son père" (p. 191) [54]. More explicit in the latter work, however, he added: "En cela il se trouvait expressément en contradiction avec Moïse, qui... assure que les enfants portent l'iniquité des pères jusqu'à la troisième et quatrième génération" (pp. 191—192) [55]. In his correspondence he would later praise the simple exposure of such contradictions as an effective way of inspiring scepticism about the authenticity of the Christian Revelation. In view of his two letters to Mme. du Deffand one may conclude that he was working on "Ezéchiel" in December 1760 and January 1761.

---

[53] "Voltaire's irony consits of adopting poses which he, and his readers, understand to be inappropriate to him, or in exploiting poses which are appropriate but dramatized for the sake of effect. These devices permit Voltaire to expose what he could never pose directly, they permit him to approach forbidden territory under cover of darkness." Peter Gay, *The Party of Humanity* (New York, 1964) p. 16.

[54] "A son is not to suffer for the sins of his father." *Ezekiel* 18:20 in *The Jerusalem Bible*.

[55] "[Yahweh] lets nothing go unchecked, punishing the father's fault in the sons and in the grandsons to the third and fourth generation." *Exodus* 34:7. This passage is quoted in part in *Numbers* 14:18. Voltaire gives the reference incorrectly as *Numbers* 28.

Since January 1760 he had been giving at least some of his attention to his "philosophical" dictionary. In his correspondence he mentioned "Idée"; alluded to "Salomon", "Christianisme" and "Ezéchiel"; went to some trouble to obtain the second two volumes of Warbuton's *Legation* which influenced several articles in the *Portatif*. Not only did he tell Mme. du Deffand that he was working on the project, but Cramer also informed Grimm that it would be forthcoming. Since these references occurred at less frequent intervals than in 1752, one may assume that he was not devoting as much time and effort to the work as in Potsdam. In a year's time, however, he probably produced considerably more material than in the two months he had spent on the work before.

After January 1761 the dictionary received less attention in his correspondence, but a letter to d'Alembert on May 7 or 8 contained a pertinent recommendation: "Ecrasez l'infâme, sans pour tant risquer de tomber comme Samson sous les ruines du temple qu'il démolit ... Renversez [les] idoles [de notre siècle] ... Frappez, et cachez votre main" (Best. 8988). In his "Histoire" Pomeau appropriately applies the final sentence to the *Portatif*. Although Voltaire did not seem to be working on it at the time, he would certainly follow his own advice in publishing it three years later.

During this interval two major concerns may have kept him from concentrating on the work as in Potsdam. To provide Marie Corneille, a poor descendant of Pierre, with an appropriate dowry, he edited an edition of the poet's works with a commentary that absorbed much of his time, energy and patience. Meanwhile, however, he was working to reverse the decision against Jean Calas, a huguenot victim of catholic fanaticism and judicial murder in Toulouse. This case inspired his *Traité sur la Tolérance* which further distracted him from preparation of his dictionary.

Nevertheless, his correspondence in the Fall of 1762 evidences a third period of activity devoted to this work. On October 10 he asked Damilaville to send him "au plus vite" (Best. 9940) François Pluquet's *Mémoire pour servir à l'histoire des égarements de l'esprit humain ... ou dictionnaire des hérésies* (1762), which d'Alembert, in an earlier letter, had ridiculed as a naïve betrayal of the "infamous". "J'ay lu le dictionnaire des hérésies", he answered d'Alembert on November 1. "Je connais quelque chose d'un peu plus fort" (Best. 9975). As Besterman comments, "something a little more daring" could only be the *Dictionnaire philosophique*. Pluquet's "dictionary of heresies" may well have served as a reference in the preparation of the "philosophical" dictionary.

On November 30 Voltaire entrusted Damilaville with an article which he had written for the work in Potsdam: "Voici ... un petit article de la lettre M d'un dictionnaire que j'avais fait pour mon usage" (Best. 10002). The claim that he had compiled the dictionary for his own use, which recalls his letter to Mme. du Deffand in 1760, should not be taken more seriously now than then. "Renvoyez moi, je vous en prie, mon *Moïse*", he wrote Damilaville the day after Christmas. "... Mon cher frère [Damilaville] voudrait il me faire avoir *presto presto,* un petit dictionnaire des conciles qui a paru, je crois, l'année passée? Cela cadrerait fort bien avec mon dictionnaire d'hérésies. La théologie m'amuse: la folie de l'esprit humain y est dans sa plénitude" (Best. 10046). His own "dictionary of heresies" reflects his amusement over the absurd positions defended by adversaries in theological controversies. He may have consulted the *Dictionnaire portatif des conciles* (Paris, 1758) by Pons Alletz for the elaboration of "Conciles", although he added this article to the *Portatif* only in 1767.

In a letter to his niece the marquise de Florian three days later, he mentioned the second Council of Nicea: "Je ... trouve [l'abbé Vincent Mignot] très-avisé, étant sous diacre, de n'avoir pas donné au concile de Nicée tous les ridicules qu'il mérite" (Best. 10049). He was referring to his nephew's "Irène", or *Histoire de l'impératrice Irène* (Amsterdam, 1762), with which he said he was otherwise "fort content". He made up for the abbé's "oversight" in "Conciles": "L'adoration des images ... fut rétablie [au second concile de Nicée]. On veut aujourd'hui justifier ce concile, en disant que cette adoration était un culte de *dulie*, et non de *latrie*" (p. 145). The Roman Catholic Church restricts *latria*, or the highest form of worship, to adoration of God, but allows *dulia*, or mere veneration, for saints and angels. Despite this distinction, the Council of Frankfort in 794, as Voltaire hastened to add, contradicted the Nicean sanction of what amounts to *idolâtrie*, which sounds like a combination of *dulie* and *latrie*. This play on words no doubt supplied the ridicule which Voltaire thought was lacking in his nephew's *Irène*. He was insinuating that the Church had tried to pass oversubtle phantasy off as divine mystery. "Pour moi", he assured his niece in the letter mentioned above, "je n'épargne pas les impertinences de l'église quand je les rencontre dans mon chemin. Je me suis fait un petit tribunal assez libre où je fais comparaître la superstition, le fanatisme, l'extravagance et la tyrannie" (Best. 10049). This small tribunal in which he dared to pass judgement on the "infamous" was probably the *Portatif.*

Without mentioning this work, he discussed the dictionary form with Elie Bertrand on 9 January 1763. Having congratulated the latter on his *Dictionnaire universel des fossiles* (The Hague, 1763) [56], he seized the opportunity to talk about such alphabetical works in general: " Il faudra d'oresnavant tout mettre en dictionaires. La vie est trop courte pour lire de suite tant de gros livres: malheur aux longues dissertations! Un dictionaire vous met sous la main dans le moment, la chose dont vous avez besoin. Ils sont utiles surtout aux persoñes déjà instruites, qui cherchent à se rappeler ce qu'ils ont sçu" (Best. 10079). It would be difficult to interpret this passage as anything other than an oblique reference to his own dictionary. He had always preferred small, accessible and practical works to thick, multi-volumed treatises as a means of disseminating his ideas. The accessibility and practicality of Bertrand's alphabetical presentation did not escape him, especially because he was preparing to exploit this popular form [57] himself. The utility of such works to readers who only wish to renew their knowledge further clarifies his own intentions. In the *Portatif* he would appeal to the majority of the reading public vaguely familiar with the Christian heritage, rather than the minority versed in the fine points of theology.

The same appeal characterizes his *Traité sur la Tolérance,* which preoccupied him during this period even more than the dictionary. Having sent Moultou the *Traité* earlier, he outlined his strategy in a letter to him on January 9: "J'ai beaucoup retravaillé l'ouvrage en question . . . il faut tâcher qu'on te lise sans dégoût; c'est par le plaisir qu'on vient à bout des hommes; répands quelques poignées de sel et d'épices dans le ragoût que tu leur présentes, mêle le ridicule aux raisons, tâche de faire naître l'indifférence, alors tu obtiendras sûrement la tolérance" (Best. 10082). The final word suggests that the

---

[56] Probably postdated.

[57] On 15 August 1764 Friedrich Grimm makes fun of another dictionary in the *Correspondance littéraire, philosophique et critique* (Paris, 1887): *"Dictionnaire domestique portatif, contenant toutes les connaissances relatives à l'économie domestique et rurale, où l'on détaille les différentes branches de l'agriculture, la manière de soiger les chevaux [etc.] par une société de gens de lettres. Je ne connais pas de meilleure plaisanterie que ce titre d'une nouvelle compilation qui vient de paraître en trois volumes. J'espère qu'incessamment une société de métayers, de laboureurs, de pêcheurs, de jardiniers, de cuisiniers, nous donnera un dictionnaire de poésie, de philosophie, de métaphysique et de morale.*" (VI, 58) This *nouvelle compilation* was therefore by no means the first the heavy-witted Grimm had seen.

"work in question" was the *Traité,* but Voltaire's description hardly suits this book. Since he had just written it the previous year, the many revisions mentioned seem more appropriate to his dictionary. He sought to amuse and insinuate in the *Portatif* rather than argue and persuade as in the *Traité.* The dictionary "recipe" was obviously the one that called for seasoning a blend of reason and ridicule with irony.

He seems to have laid the project aside once again, however, for it disappeared from his correspondence at this point. In a scant two months he had examined three significant works, two of which resemble his dictionary by their form and two of which provide information about his subject matter. He had also sent an article from the Potsdam period to Damilaville and even discussed his project, though obliquely, with various correspondents. But his progress was presumably small in comparison to the two previous periods of activity specifically related to the *Portatif.*

Despite his extraordinary energy, it is unlikely that he could have produced the contents of the 344 pages in the first edition during these three periods, even with the aid of the materials he had accumulated during his stay at the Abbey of Senones and during the Cirey period. Even if he worked quietly on an occasional article at other times, he probably would not have had the manuscript ready for Cramer by the summer of 1764 without a final burst of energy. Although his correspondence presents little evidence of such activity, his work load appears to have decreased during the second half of 1763. In fact Besterman describes the last four months of this year as "singularly uneventful" [58].

There is at least one sure indication that he was not neglecting the dictionary. "Je vous ay demandé trois fois le mss de l'article idolâtrie que frère Platon [Diderot] doit avoir, et dont j'ay un besoin pressant", he wrote Damilaville on 23 May 1763. We have no record of these three requests, unless Voltaire was referring to the crisis of 1757 when, in support of d'Alembert's resignation as co-editor of the Encyclopedia, he had insisted on the return of his articles. He asked Damilaville for "Idolâtrie" again on May 25, but on May 28 he told him: "Je retrouve l'article *idolâtrie.* Ainsi voilà de la peine épargnée pour frère Platon" (Best. 10415). Apparently he had found a copy of the manuscript in his papers. But why did he need the article so badly at this time? Since no work known to have been written by

---

[58] *Correspondence,* LIII, xxiii.

him during the period duplicates the information in "Idolâtrie", one may presume that he wanted the article for the final revision of his dictionary.

In order to understand his maneuvers after publication of this work a year later, it is convenient to examine another question he raised in 1763. A Paris book peddler was selling a new edition of his *Essai sur l'Histoire générale* — a consolidation of the *Essai sur les Moeurs* (1756) and the *Siècle de Louis XIV* (1751) — with his name on the titlepage. This situation alarmed him because the government regarded by-lines in questionable works as an open defiance of its authority and it challenged almost any work by Voltaire. "Quand l'auteur avait eu l'audace de signer son oeuvre", states Belin, "il pouvait être décrété de prise de corps ou emprisonné [59]." Voltaire protested accordingly to Damilaville on June 23:

> Tout ce que j'ay souhaitté c'est que mon nom ne parût pas. Car en vérité il m'importe assez peu que le livre soit condamné ou non. On a tant brûlé de livres bons ou mauvais … tant d'ouvrages dévots ou impies, que cela ne fait plus la moindre sensation … Mais pour la personne de l'auteur c'est autre chose. Je ne voudrais pas être obligé de désavouer mon ouvrage comme Helvétius. On ne peut jamais procéder que contre le livre, et contre l'auteur … on ordonera des recherches, on n'en fera pas à Ferney ou aux Délices.   (Best. 10457)

"Frappez et cachez votre main" (Best. 8988), he had advised d'Alembert in 1761. Books are expendable; spare the author. Quarrels between his Jansenist and Jesuit enemies had resulted in the burning of many works in public. This judicial ceremony had in fact been abused so frequently that it no longer had much impact on public opinion. Proof of authorship, on the other hand, must be denied the authorities at all costs [60]. They could do little to a writer of Voltaire's reputation as long as he did not compromise the support of influential friends by imprudence or impudence. They would prevent any search of his premises by officers of the law. Voltaire's remark about Helvétius, who had been forced to repudiate *De l'Esprit* in 1758, is also

---

[59] J.-P. Belin, *le Commerce des livres prohibés à Paris de 1750 à 1789* (New York, 1913), p. 114.

[60] Concerning the *Histoire générale* he asks the d'Argentals: "Je vous supplie de m'instruire si les Crammer ont laissé subsisté mon nom à la tête de quelques exemplaires. Ce point est très important, car on ne peut procéder contre la personne, que quand elle s'est nommée. Toutes les procédures générales et sans objet, tombent." (Best. 10462).

interesting. At the time Voltaire had concluded, as usual, that one must not risk the publication of such "philosophical" works in France. But here he concluded that he would not like to find himself in the same predicament.

At the moment, however, he felt safe. Six days after his letter to Damilaville, he displayed even greater confidence in his security. "Je n'habite point en France", he assured the d'Argentals, "je n'ay rien en France qu'on puisse saisir, j'ay un petit fonds pour les temps d'orage. Je répète que le parlement ne peut rien sur ma fortune, ny sur ma personne ny sur mon âme" (Best. 10462). Living almost exclusively at Ferney by 1763 [61], he considered this fief independent of France, a strangely feudal claim. Paris was several hundred miles away and the Genevan border, only a few hundred yards, a situation that had influenced his decision to buy the property. Should he flee he could expect to receive an income wherever he went from the annuity he had purchased from the duke of Wurttemberg for such a "rainy day". As for his enemies in the Paris Parlement, one wonders if he really thought he was financially, personally and psychically beyond their reach. His "soul", which he threw in as a joke here, would prove most vulnerable to their vengeance.

Such an idea was far from his thoughts when in that same letter to the d'Argentals he expressed his impatience to witness the collapse of religious tyranny. This sense of urgency stemmed in part from his dwindling life-expectancy and in part from a rebirth of "adolescent" enthusiasm: "Voicy le temps où mon sang bout, voicy le temps de faire quelque chose. Il faut se presser, l'âge avance. Il n'y a pas un moment à perdre ... Ce n'est pas assez d'être un vieil acteur [62]. Je suis et je dois être un vieil auteur, car il faut remplir sa destinée jusqu'au dernier moment" (Best. 10462). Yearning to be remembered not only as an author, but also as an actor, he thus felt that he was on the verge of accomplishing a destiny that his contemporaries had already conceded to him. Although he may have been thinking of the stage in particular, role-playing was also a part of his writing career. Refusing to resign himself to the usual consequences of being sixty-nine years old, he therefore annouced a decisive act that would leave his mark on history.

---

[61] "He lives now entirely at Ferney." (Best. 10520 from Gibbon to Dorothea Gibbon on 6 Aug. 1763).

[62] In 1763 Edward Gibbon described Voltaire's acting as follows: "Either my taste is improved or Voltaire's talents are impaired since I last saw him: He appeared to me now a very ranting unnatural performer." (Best. 10520).

Confidence and enthusiasm were apparently whetting his impatience to achieve this goal when on September 15 he wrote Helvétius as follows: "[La] raison tant persécutée gagne tous les jours du terrain. On a beau faire, il arrivera en France chez les honnêtes gens ce qui est arrivé en Angleterre ... Nous prenons insensiblement leur noble liberté de penser, et leur profond mépris pour les fadaises de L'école. Les jeunes gens se forment, ceux qui sont destinez aux plus grandes places sont défaits des infâmes préjugez qui avilissent une nation" (Best. 10595). His optimism recalls the *Lettres philosophiques* (1734), which he had written on the assumption that France would eventually profit from England's example of intellectual progress and freedom. Perhaps in 1763 he really believed that reason and free thought were winning over persecution and authority. A little rashly he assumed that the nation's youth would consolidate this victory because they did not share in their parents' prejudices. He even insisted that "notre party l'emporte sur le leur dans la bonne compagnie" (Best. 10595). Since the most influential members of society were "good company" in eighteenth-century France, his remark is almost categorical. There can be little doubt that his optimism, which appears in much of the correspondence from the second half of 1763 and some from the first half of 1764, was riding on expectations that the dictionary would soon be published.

In a letter to Helvétius on October 4 he explained a tactic that he was using in this work: "Il y a une belle histoire à faire, c'est celle des contradictions ... [qui] règnent depuis Luc et Matthieu, ou plutôt depuis Moïse. Ce serait une chose bien curieuse que de mettre sous les yeux ce scandale de l'esprit humain" (Best. 10618). Actually this *belle histoire* was no longer *à faire* since he was probably readying it for publication at the time. He went on to tell Helvétius some of the contradictions he had discovered in the Bible and two of these examples also appeared in "Moïse": (1) In *Exodus* Moses says in 33:11 that he saw God face to face and in 33:20,23 that he only saw Him from the rear [63]; (2) in *Leviticus* 20:21 he prescribes marriage

---

[63] "Moyse dit qu'il a vu Dieu face à face et qu'il ne l'a vu que par derrière." (Best. 10618) In "Moïse" Voltaire had the Children of Israel protest to Moses: "Tantôt [vous] nous dites que vous avez parlé avec Dieu face à face, et tantôt que vous n'avez pu le voir que par derrière!" (p. 324) *The Jerusalem Bible* gives these passages as follows: "Yahweh would speak with Moses face to face, as a man speaks with his friend" (33:11)" 'You cannot see my face', he said, 'for man cannot see and live.'" (33:20) "Then I will take my hand away and you shall see the back of me; but my face is not to be seen." (33:23).

to one's sister-in-law, a marriage he prohibits in *Deuteronomy* 25:5 [64]. Such recollection of specific examples from an article written eleven years earlier in Potsdam suggests that he was revising it in 1763. By exposing these and more serious contradictions in the *Portatif* he would infuriate pious Christians who refused to admit any kind of error in the Holy Scriptures. The resulting scandal would publicize the work as usual. And the work itself would be an open invitation to examine such contradictions critically, an examination that could only weaken the authority of the "infamous".

Or even destroy it. "Il est clair", he wrote Damilaville the same day, "qu'il faut nétoier la place avant de bâtir, et qu'on doit commencer par démolir l'ancien édifice, élevé dans les temps barbares" (Best. 10619). In the *Portatif* he emphasized the "barbarity" of the "edifice" by exhibiting aspects of the *Bible* and sacred history likely to revolt his refined contemporaries, such as Ezekiel's "lunch". One should not interpret his allusion to "petits ouvrages" in the letter as limited to *rogatons, facéties, épîtres* and the like, for his dictionary would be composed of "petits chapitres", as he was fond of calling them. He may have mentioned small works to deceive Damilaville's friends the Encyclopedists. At any rate, demolition of the old order to make room for the new would require powerful explosive. He went on in the letter to express his habitual scepticism about the utility of metaphysical treatises: "Les ouvrages métaphysiques sont lus de peu de personnes, et trouvent toujours des contradicteurs. Les faits évidents, les choses simples et claires, sont à la portée de tout le monde et font un éffet immanquable" (Best. 10619). Such works attracted critics rather than readers, while facts clearly and simply stated had strong appeal for the general reading public. Although Voltaire appeared to be exhorting the Encyclopedists to engage in this "philosophical" activity, he was fully aware that his own *Portatif* would meet all of these specifications.

Elation accompanies such exhortations in his correspondence after November 22 when the French Academy elected Marmontel to membership, an important victory for "philosophy". "Nous touchons au

---

[64] "[Moïse] défend qu'on épouse sa bellesoeur; et il ordonne qu'on épouse sa bellesoeur." (Best. 10618) "Le *Lévitique* défend d'épouser la femme de son frère, le *Deutéronome* l'ordonne." (p. 322) "The man who takes to wife the wife of his brother: that is impurity; he has uncovered his brother's nakedness, and they shall die childless." (*Leviticus* 20:21) "If brothers live together and one of them dies childless, the dead man's wife must not marry a stranger outside the family." (*Deuteronomy* 25:5).

temps où les hommes vont commencer à devenir raisonnables", he wrote d'Alembert on December 13. "Les hommes qui gouvernent ou qui sont nés pour le gouvernement ... les gens de lettres dignes de ce nom ... Je suis enchanté que m. Marmontel soit notre confrère [à l'Académie]" (Best. 10718). The assumption that men of one's own sort were best fitted to govern [65] was of course an illusion, but Voltaire had good reason to believe himself superior to other men. That he had never been called to participate in any government, except for a few diplomatic chores, may have been a disappointment, and now it was too late. The advent of a more reasonable epoch would nevertheless favor his attempt to leave his mark on history.

His optimism continued into 1764, but there is no positive evidence that he was still working on his dictionary. Specific allusions to "Idolâtrie", written for the Encyclopedia, and "Moïse", composed in Potsdam, suggest that he was revising it during the second half of 1763. Exhortations addressed to his "philosophical brothers" seem to indicate that he was preparing it for publication at what he thought would be a turning point in the struggle against intellectual tyranny. The lack of more explicit reference does not necessarily weaken this theory, because he fully understood the value of surprise and, if past experience meant anything, he could expect a violent reaction to such a work. Silence was golden for the moment.

Reticence about the *Portatif* during the first half of 1764 did not prevent him from expressing his impatience with the delay of the final decision in the Calas affair, for which he was probably delaying publication. Nor did it impede his enthusiasm for the role of the Hiérophante in his tragedy *Olympie*, first performed at Ferney in 1762. "J'ai représenté ce personnage, moi qui vous parle", he wrote the d'Argentals on March 11. "J'avais une grande barbe blanche avec une mitre de deux pieds de haut, et un manteau beaucoup plus beau que celui d'Aaron. Mais quelle onction était dans mes paroles! Je faisais pleurer les petits garçon" (Best. 10921). Let us recall the earlier letter to the d'Argentals in which he said his blood was boiling to accomplish his destiny both as a writer and an actor. Ridgeway describes the Hiéophante as an

apostle of *bienfaisance* and enlightened minister of a god of clemency ... Voltaire ... thought of himself as the prophet of a new,

---

[65] "C'est l'interest du roy, c'est celui de l'état que les philosophes gouvernent la société. Ils inspirent l'amour de la patrie et les fanatiques y portent le trouble." (Best. 10595).

universal religion, a kind of minimum creed, acceptable to all reasonable men. And for all his ferocious attacks on clerical intolerance, bigotry and fanaticism, [he] had no desire to see the priesthood abolished. In the *Dictionnaire philosophique* ... he makes it clear that priests have an important function in his ideal society [66].

One wonders in fact if this commonsense assault on religious mystery was not assuming the proportions of a sacred work in his mind, however incongruous that may seem. His outburst of enthusiasm for the role of the aging prophet apparently belongs to the great expectations of 1764. Perhaps he thought his literary and dramatic talents were converging at the apex of an "evangelical" career.

Would they not precipitate a great act? "Je songe à porter les derniers coups à l'infâme" (Best. 11058), he announced in a letter to Damilaville on May 28. Several factors must have been contributing to this conviction that he could soon slay the dragon. Marmontel's election to the Academy was certainly one of them. The continuing persecution of the once powerful Jesuits was probably another. But the reversal of the Calas decision was, to Voltaire's mind, decisive. "L'arrêt par lequel on avait roué Calas a été cassé d'une voix unanime", he informed Gabriel Cramer on June 7 or 8. "Mais les os de ce pauvre Calas n'en ont pas été moins cassées" (Best. 11075). This morbid pun may well have been a signal to his eager publisher to go ahead with the distribution of the *Traité sur la Tolérance* and the printing of the *Dictionnaire philosophique portatif*. Voltaire had allowed copies of the *Traité* to reach only his friends for fear of jeopardizing the judical proceedings that would eventually reinstate Calas. The same motive would explain the opportune appearance of the *Portatif* in July. It would also explain his loud expectations in the second half of 1763 and his quiet expectations in the first half of 1764. One imagines that he had put the final touches on the manuscript of the dictionary in December, then postponed publication until he had received news of the Calas decision.

Less than a week had gone by when he wrote Damilaville: "Je n'ai pas de temps à perdre. L'infâme m'occupe assez" (Best. 11085). Was he correcting proofs? In ten days he was telling the d'Argentals how the Calas affair and the *Traité sur la Tolérance* were enlightening public opinion. Biblically, he concludes: "Le règne de la vérité est proche" (Best. 11094). His letters also reveal that Gabriel Cramer left for Paris either on this day (June 17) or the next [67]. On July 6

---

[66] "Voltaire as an Actor," p. 276.

he sent still another letter to Damilaville, which shows that Cramer had finished printing the *Portatif* before leaving Geneva.

> Je me doute bien de ce que frère Cramer vous montrera, mais je ne crois pas que cet ouvrage doive jamais être vendu avec privilège. Je vous demande en grâce de confondre tout barbare et tout faux frère qui pourait me soupçonner d'avoir mis la main à ce saint oeuvre. Je veux le bien de l'église; mais je renonce de tout mon coeur au martire.   (Best. 11137)

There can be no doubt that Voltaire had asked Cramer to show his friends in Paris a copy of the freshly printed *Portatif*. His language clearly indicates that Damilaville had not seen the work before, that it would be controversial and that Voltaire would as usual deny his authorship. His renunciation of martyrdom is also typical. The nature of the church he mentions emerges in the next sentence (unquoted here), where he considers his *Extrait des sentiments de Jean Meslier* (1762) a holy writ that had won many converts to the new belief (or disbelief). Since he thought of the *Portatif* as a sort of "philosophical" gospel, his use of religious terminology in this letter may have been only half ironical.

The work was apparently the subject of correspondence between Voltaire and Cramer which has since been lost. The *Mémoires secrets* give Cramer himself as the source of the following anecdote: The publisher wrote Voltaire "pour lui rendre compte d'un livre nouveau, fort scandaleux, qui faisait grand bruit à Paris, et qu'on lui attribuait ... il lui priait de vouloir bien lui en envoyer un exemplaire" (II, 79). Voltaire replied that he had also heard of the *Dictionnaire philosophique*, that he had not read it and that he would appreciate Cramer's sending him a copy should he find one. Cramer wrote back that he had shown Voltaire's letter to everyone, as he assumed the latter expected him to. Except for details omitted here, Jean Louis Wagnière, Voltaire's secretary during the later years, confirms this naïve accont in his "Examen des *Mémoires secrets*". "M. de Voltaire et son libraire étaient pourvus du livre, mais il avait été convenu entre eux d'écrire ces lettres ostensibles" [68]. They took this precaution, Wagnière explains, to provide each other with evidence tending to

---

[67] On June 20 Voltaire wrote Damilaville that "St. Paul s'était brouillé avec Gamaliel, parce que ce Gamaliel lui avait refusé sa fille." (Best. 11102) This assertion occurs in the article "Paul", which he would insert in the *Portatif* in 1765.

[68] *Mémoires sur Voltaire* (Paris, 1826), I, 223.

prove their innocence in case of trouble with the authorities. This comic procedure smacks of Voltaire's inclination for play-acting.

The advance copy of the work that Cramer was showing his friends in Paris brought immediate requests for copies from Damilaville and d'Alembert. In answering them Voltaire's first impulse was to assure them that he had not written it. He did promise them copies as soon as he could find the work, as if he did not know where to look! "Celà sent terriblement le fagot" (Best. 11140), he confided in Damilaville on July 9. "J'ai ouï parler de ce petit abominable dictionnaire" (Best. 11149), he told d'Alembert on July 16. News of the "abominable dictionary" and its author, who had fooled almost no one, was spreading fast. In view of "la liberté qui règne sur cet écrit & le nom imposant de son auteur" (II, 79), proclaimed the *Mémoires secrets,* the police would be seeking it out as avidly as the reading public, a prediction that would soon prove true.

Their motives were of course mutually antagonistic and reciprocally compelling, for curiosity provoked severer censorship and censorship excited greater curiosity. Since this circle was particularly vicious in Paris, a few copies of the *Portatif* smuggled into that great cultural center were enough to provoke a scandal that reverberated throughout Europe. Such publicity was both cheap and pervasive. If the author were unknown, or even if important people professed to believe him anonymous, he would escape punishment. But Voltaire had long since learned that, by vociferously denying his authorship, he could obtain even greater publicity, and especially in Paris where most of his correspondents lived.

By September 1, when Grimm announced the *Portatif* in his *Correspondance littéraire* [69], only a small number of copies had reached Paris: "Il existe un *Dictionnaire philosophique portatif* ... publié par le zèle infatigable du patriarche des Délices; mais cela n'est vrai que pour les vrais fidèles, car pour les malveillants, il est démontré que ce grand apôtre n'y a aucune part. Au reste, l'édition entière de cet évangile précieux se réduit à vingt ou vingt-cinq exemplaires" (VI, 65). His irony about the identity of the author demonstrates to what extent he believed Voltaire's denials of responsibility and heeded his pleas not to attribute the work to him. Grimm's estimate of from twenty to twenty-five copies probably came from a reliable source, perhaps Cramer himself, because Voltaire wrote d'Alembert on Octo-

---

[69] This periodical existed only in manuscript form at the time and was distributed to Grimm's aristocratic correspondents in foreign countries.

ber 19 that "il y ... a peu d'exemplaires à Paris, et ... ils ne sont guère qu'entre les mains des adeptes. J'ai empêché jusqu'ici qu'il n'en entrât davantage" (Best. 11310). Distributing only a few copies to the "adept" had the effect of teasing public curiosity and testing official reaction to the work.

Official reaction came more swiftly in Geneva than Paris. The Attorney General Jean Robert Tronchin [70] reported the dictionary to the ruling Petit Conseil on September 10 and presented them with an indictment of it on September 20:

> Ce n'est point un Systême ... qui séduit difficilement cet ordre nom-il soumet quelques uns de ses Dogmes les plus importans à la plus audacieuse critique; Il l'attaque dans ses Monumens historiques, dans les Miracles sur lesquels elle s'appuye; Il rassemble avec complaisance contre ces miracles les objections qu'il croit les plus redoutables, il leur donne une piquante tournure, et il ne les résout qu'en paroissant soumettre sa Raison à une Foi dont il a essayé de rendre l'objet impossible et ridicule; Comme si la sagesse Divine pouvoit prescrire une croyance qui scandalisât le Bon sens.   (Best. 11255)

This frigid and incisive analysis clearly revealed Voltaire's basic technique in the *Portatif:* submitting articles of faith to a common-sense scrutiny and then, having exposed them to ridicule, resigning himself ironically to spiritual authority. Let us not be fooled by Tronchin's acceptance of the author's anonymity. As Attorney General he had no proof, but as Rousseau's enemy in the *Lettres de la Campagne* (1763), he could hardly have failed to recognize the hand of another religious renegade, a man he knew and who lived only a few miles away. Nor did Voltaire's intention in using alphabetical order escape the implacable Tronchin:

> Ce n'est point un Systême ... qui séduit difficilement cet ordre nombreux de lecteurs hors d'état de suivre la Chaine des idées ... Ce sont des Articles détachés, dont l'arrangement commode leur laisse la malheureuse facilité d'y trouver ce qui peut les flatter le plus, et qui est le plus proportionné au degré de leur intelligence.   (Best. 11255)

Thus Tronchin denounced Voltaire's efforts to reach a much larger public than the usual specialists and intellectuals as an attempt to subvert the masses. In his preface to the 1765 edition published by

---

[70] Not to be confused with Voltaire's friend the banker who had exactly the same name.

Varberg in Amsterdam, Voltaire would praise what Tronchin had deplored: "Les personnes de tout état trouveront de quoi s'instruire en s'amusant. Ce livre n'exige pas une lecture suivie; mais à quelque endroit qu'on l'ouvre, on trouve de quoi réfléchir" [71]. Voltaire's approval and Tronchin's disapproval of the same phenomenon illustrate the contrast between their respective attitudes towards human reason. Voltaire had confidence in it, while Tronchin was suspicious of it. Fortunately, the Attorney General did not choose to pursue the matter further. For fear of giving the work too much publicity and out of deference perhaps to Voltaire, he asked the Conseil not to deal too severely with the book. Had he wished to persecute the author, he would have been a dangerous enemy.

Meanwhile, Voltaire had initiated a letter-writing campaign to deny his authorship and confuse the issue, a tactic he had developed during his long career in clandestine publication. As usual, he took pains to adapt each letter to the mentality of the addressee. To the président Hénault, a former member of the Paris Parlament who had ties with the Queen and the pious faction, he denied all responsibility for the *Portatif* on October 20, admitting only that: L'éditeur a mis dans l'ouvrage une demi-douzaine de morceaux que j'avais destinés autrefois au dictionnaire encyclopédique [l'*Encyclopédie*]" (Best. 11320). In this way he provided the flexible Hénault with a sly argument to placate his enemies. To d'Alembert, a fellow free-thinker and faint-hearted disciple, he admitted some responsibility on October 12: "Quelques personnes ont rassemblé ces matériaux, et je puis y avoir eu quelque part" (Best. 11298). Thus the old idea of organizing his own collective enterprise re-emerges, furnishing d'Alembert with an argument to persuade his friends that the *Portatif* was his dream come true. He knew that both Hénault and d'Alembert would talk, that conflicting rumors would circulate and that both his name and his work would receive much publicity. He also hoped no doubt that the resulting confusion would hamper the police.

He denied his responsibility for the work in at least sixty letters written over the last three months of 1764 and the first three months of 1765. The epithets he used for the title appear to condemn it: *ce dictionnaire diabolique, un ouvrage anti-chrétien, cette abominable production* (Best. 11236 to d'Alembert), *ce diabolique ouvrage, cette oeuvre infernale* (Best. 11246 to the d'Argentals), *un livre diabolique, ces oeuvres de Sathan* (Best. 11264 to Mme. d'Epinay), *un livre infernal,*

---

[71] 1967 edition, p. XXXII.

ce livre affreux (Best. 11324 to Richelieu). But he knew these "philosophical" friends would interpret the adjective "diabolical" [72] and its equivalents as "anti-christian", an interpretation confirmed by the phrase quoted from his letter to d'Alembert above (Best. 11236). From such enemies of "superstition" this language elicited approval of the work rather than condemnation. Occasionally, he expressed himself more openly, as in a letter to Mme. du Deffand on October 8: "En général, le livre inspire de la vertu, et rend toutes les superstitions détestables" (Best. 11291). In praising the book, however, he always pretended that someone else had written it [73].

Although he never tired of echoing his innocence, he had recourse to a variety of more subtle maneuvers tested in earlier campaigns. In his letter to Hénault on October 20, for instance, his hypochondria provided a typical excuse: "Je pourrais si je voulais me plaindre qu'à l'âge de 71 ans, accablé d'infirmités et presque aveugle [74] on ne veuille pas me laisser achever ma carrière en paix; mais je ne suis pas assez sot pour me plaindre" (Best. 11320). In this way he implied that he would have no reason to invite trouble by publishing such a dangerous work [75]. Another emotional appeal, which he used less frequently, appears in his letter to d'Alembert on October 12: "C'était uniquement dans la vue de tirer une famille nombreuse de la plus affreuse misère. Le père avait une mauvaise petite imprimerie" (Best. 11298). This claim was not as ridiculous as it may sound since Voltaire had contributed the royalties from the *Traité sur la Tolérance* to the survivors of the Calas family. But Gabriel Cramer, who was prospering from the publication of his works, hardly fitted the description. This playful lie, which certainly did not fool d'Alembert, had the advantage of drawing attention to someone, albeit imaginary, more worthy of pity than himself.

---

[72] Since Voltaire had claimed many times that the work was *de plusieurs mains*, d'Alembert replied: "Il est évident, comme vous dites, que l'ouvrage est de différentes mains; pour moi j'y en ai reconnu au moins quatre, celles de Belzebuth, d'Astaroth, de Lucifer, et d'Asmodée" (Best. 11286 on October 4).

[73] "V. s'enveloppe dans son innocence" (Best. 11334), he admitted to the comte d'Argental on November 2. He was adapting Horace's *Ode* III, xxix, 29—30: "Prudens futuri temporis exitum [caliginosa nocte premit deus] ridetque".

[74] When he composed this letter, his vision was impaired by an inflammation of the eyes which glare from the snow would later aggravate.

[75] "Vous me demandez pourquoi je m'inquiète tant sur un livre auquel je n'ai nulle part ... c'est qu'à l'âge de soixante et onze ans, malade et presque aveugle, je suis prêt à essuyer la persécution la plus violente; c'est qu'enfin je ne veux pas mourir martyr d'un livre que je n'ai pas fait" (Best. 11310 to d'Alembert on Oct. 19).

He complemented such sentimental diversions by technical ones. Deploring the shoddy printing in an edition he wished to disown had always been a favorite trick: "[Le *Portatif*] est ... horriblement mal imprimé et rempli de fautes absurdes", he wrote the marquise de Jaucourt on October 3. "Il y aurait bien de la malignité à m'imputer cette rapsodie" (Best. 11285). Certainly he would have nothing to do with an edition so badly printed that it would hurt his reputation as a writer!

A more cunning tactic was to sow rumors about places of publication other than the authentic ones. He mentioned Holland frequently, for everyone knew that Huguenot immigrants there were publishing a great many works prohibited in France. Towards the end of November, Marc Michel Rey in Amsterdam would in fact publish the second edition of the *Portatif* to have Voltaire's secret blessing. Voltaire also cited the Hague, Liège, Basel and Rouen. On October 1 he told the d'Argentals that he had taken action to "empêcher un scélérat de libraire nommé Besongne, natif de Normandie, d'imprimer l'infernale" (Best. 11277). He was not making a play on words (Besongne and *besogne*) since there actually was such a publisher in Rouen specializing in the *genre de prohibé* [76]. In other correspondence he asked Bordes to see whether an edition was being printed in Lyon and informed Elie Bertrand that he had procured a copy from Frankfurt. In a letter to the comte d'Argental he named Lausanne as the address of the poor printer whose large family the opportunity had saved from misery. He omitted London, a favorite place of publication, ficticious or authentic, probably because both of his 1764 editions of the *Portatif* claim to have been printed there. If such lies became rumors and spread as one might expect, they had the effect of proliferating editions of the scandalous work. His enemies and officials regulating the book trade must have felt as if they were facing a hydra.

This trick by no means emptied Voltaire's bag. His earlier collaboration on the Encyclopedia inspired the claim that the *Portatif* consisted mostly of unused articles which he and other collaborators had contributed to that work: "La plupart des articles étaient destinés à l'enciclopédie, par quelques gens de lettres, dont les originaux sont encore entre les mains de Briasson" [77], he assured the comtesse d'Ar-

---

[76] In his *Commerce,* Belin says: "A Rouen trois imprimeurs s'étaient spécialisés dans le genre de prohibé [dont] Besongne" (p. 51).

[77] One of the three publishers of the *Encyclopédie.*

gental in early November. "S'il y a quelques articles de moi, comme Amitié, Amour, Anthropophages, Caractère, la Chine, Fraude, Gloire[78], Guerre, Lois, Luxe, Vertu, je ne dois répondre en aucune façon des autres" (Best. 11341). In a letter to the comte d'Argental on October 20 he also mentioned "Amour-propre", "Amour socratique" and "Amitié". All of these articles appear in the *Portatif*, and none in the *Encyclopédie*. In other correspondence he acknowledged the two articles that do figure in both works, "Messie" and "Idole, Idolâtre, Idolâtrie". Both titles appear for instance in letters to d'Alembert. To someone in a position to know what he had actually contributed to the Encyclopedia, he therefore told the truth, but few were in this position. To others he lied abundantly, accepting some of the titles in the *Portatif* only as articles he had written for the *Encyclopédie* and denying the others as the work of fellow collaborators on the latter work. This mixture of truth and falsehood could be expected to diversify responsibility for the dictionary and cause the usual conflicting rumors. It could also be expected to reassure Voltaire's friendly "rivals" the Encyclopedists, persuade his other friends or at least supply them with an argument in his defense and complicate the task of enemies bent on punishing him. All the talk would produce greater publicity for the work.

Hoping no doubt to make it more believable, he tried to persuade his fellow Encyclopedists to support his claims of innocence on the grounds that association with the *Portatif* would tarnish the reputation of the *Encyclopédie*. "Rien ne serait... plus dangereux pour l'enciclopédie", he wrote Damilaville on September 29, "que l'imputation d'un dictionaire philosophique, à un homme qui a travaillé quelquefois pour l'enciclopédie même" (Best 11270). Once again, this appeal was not so ridiculous as it may seem, for guilt by association with Helvétius' *Esprit* had contributed to the condemnation of the *Encyclopédie* in 1759. No one, however, and perhaps Voltaire least of all, appears to have taken this attempt to hide under the skirts of the Encyclopedia [79] seriously.

---

[78] He had already published this article in his *Mélanges* in 1741. It would eventually appear in the *Questions*.

[79] The following sentence from an undated letter to the marquise de Jaucourt is another example: "Comme mr de Jaucourt veut bien travailler à l'enciclopédie, et que la persécution excitée contre le dictionaire pilosophique peut s'étendre jusqu'au dictionaire de l'enciclopédie, il y a quelque intérêt de connaître et de faire voir combien on a tort de m'imputer le petit dictionaire en question" (Best. 11314).

Yet he tried to implicate the Encyclopedia in a more compromising way. "Messie" in the *Portatif*, he insisted, was the same as the "Messie" that Polier de Bottens had written for the *Encyclopédie*. Actually Voltaire had encouraged Polier to write the article for the Encyclopedia, and then rewrote it himself for his dictionary. In "Voltaire and Polier de Bottens" [80] Torrey and Wade conclude: "The ponderous, bulky and somewhat overweighted article of Polier was reduced to the short, rapid and light proportions of a normal Voltaire article ... When one considers how little was left of the original contribution one must conclude that Voltaire was really publishing his own work." (p. 155) In letters to d'Alembert and Damilaville on October 12, Voltaire nevertheless attributed the "Messie" in the *Portatif* to Polier. "Mr Polier ... envoia ce morceau avec plusieurs autres à Briasson, qui doit avoir l'original", he told d'Alembert. "Il était destiné à l'enciclopédie" (Best. 11298). And Damilaville: "L'original est encor entre mes mains, et on en avait envoyé une copie il y a cinq ou six ans aux libraires de l'enciclopédie" (Best. 11299) Voltaire must have found the manuscript between the first and the second letters. On October 22 he informed the comte d'Argental that "deux conseillers du conseil de Genêve sont venus dîner aujourd'hui chez moi; ils ont constaté que le Dictionnaire philosophique qu'on m'impute est de plusieurs mains, ils ont reconnu l'écriture et la signature de l'auteur de l'article Messie" (Best. 11323). These and other "preuves démonstratives" [81] apparently convinced the councilmen, since Voltaire continued to attribute "Messie" to Polier without bothering to mention his "proof". Only a month earlier the Attorney General of Geneva had presented his indictment of the *Portatif* to presumably the same council. For the moment at least Voltaire's maneuver seems to have allayed the danger from just across the border.

Polier is only one of several writers to whom he ascribed articles in his dictionary. Between 12 October 1764 and 4 January 1765, he named Fernand Abauzit eight times as the author of "Apocalypse" and twice as having written a part of "Christianisme". He also gave "Christianisme" twice to Warburton. Three times he attributed "Enfer" to Warburton and once, "Baptême", to Conyers Middleton. To reinforce these claims he composed a memoir [82] reaffirming all of them, except that Warbuton received "Christianisme". In this

---

[80] *Romanic Review*, XXXI, 147—155.
[81] Best. 11339 to the comte d'Argental on November 5.

document he also mentioned "Messie" with its original author Polier as well as "Amour", "Amitié", "Guerre" and "Gloire" without theirs. A young man in Switzerland, he said, had collected these and other articles intended for the Encyclopedia and had published them in Basel. The memoir included a few corrections of statistical errors, a scornful appraisal of the paper and the printing, the usual plea to absolve Voltaire of any responsibility. Letters to the marquise de Jaucourt (undated) and Damilaville (October 19) reveal that he had enclosed copies of the memoir. "Je joins ici un petit mémoire", he explained to Damilaville, "que je vous prie d'envoyer à Briasson pour le communiquer aux encyclopédistes" (Best. 11313). It is reasonable to assume that it accompanied many of his other letters as well.

On October 20 he wrote Charles Duclos, *secrétaire perpétuel* of the French Academy, asking to be exonerated of responsibility for the work of several authors. The letter was read a week later before twelve of his fellow members, most of them sympathetic to him[83]. The *Mémoires secrets* report this reading and Wagnière comments: "On avait mandé de Paris à M. *de Voltaire* que l'on travaillait à obtenir contre lui une lettre de cachet, comme auteur du *Dictionnaire philosophique*" (I, 225). His appeal to the Academy may have provided his defenders with an effective argument against this attempt to emprison him arbitrarily. In a letter to the comtesse d'Argental in early November, he gloats: "L'ouvrage est de plusieurs mains . . . C'est le sentiment de toute l'académie. Je lui en ai écrit par le secré-taire perpétuel. Quelques académiciens qui avaient vu les originaux chez Briasson, ont certifié une vérité qui m'est essentielle" (Best. 11341). But "several academicians" were not "the entire academy". Furthermore, "the entire academy" was unlikely to grant such a favor to a "philosopher" and, if "several academicians" had accepted to certify a pack of lies, they were his friends. In any case the registers of the Academy indicate no such action. In thanking d'Alem-bert on November 9 for his possible intervention, Voltaire himself seems to have realized that he had received no official endorsement from his fellow "immortals": "C'est vous, sans doute . . . qui avez certifié que cet ouvrage est de plusieurs mains" (Best. 11346).

---

[82] Appendix 166 in Besterman's *Correspondence*, LVI, 289—290.

[83] Among those present according to the *Registres de l'Académie Française* (Paris, 1895), d'Alembert, Dortous de Mairan, the abbés d'Olivet and de Voisenon, Saurin, Chateaubrun, Sainte-Pelaye and Watelet could be expected to support Voltaire on such an occasion. The abbé Trublet and Duclos himself were doubtful supporters, while the abbé Batteux and Foncemagne were his enemies.

Between October 12 and November 9 he had written that "[Le *Portatif*] est de plusieurs mains" fourteen times and three times in a single letter [84]. This obsession harked back to his old dream of directing a collective enterprise like the *Encyclopédie*. The former Encyclopedists who composed the articles in the *Portatif*, he said, had formed a society of their own for this purpose. In early November he told the comtesse d'Argental: "Il faut bénir le siècle où nous vivons qu'il se soit trouvé une société de gens de lettres et dans cette société des prêtres qui prêchent le sens commun. Mais enfin je ne dois pas m'approprier ce qui n'est pas de moi" (Best. 11341). While seeking greater safety in numbers [85], he would also enjoy the spiritual leadership of such a group. He had never realized this ambition, but he seems to have resuscitated it to protect himself from retaliation against the *Portatif*.

His claim that it contained works by several other authors was of course false, even though he had borrowed extensively from those he mentioned. In her "Voltaire and Fernand Abauzit" [86], Mina Waterman proves that he derived "Apocalypse" from a manuscript of Abauzit's *Discours historique et critique sur l'Apocalypse* (1770). In *Voltaire and the English Deists* (New Haven, 1967) Norman Torrey states that Warburton's *Divine Legation* inspired "Enfer" and Middleton's *Essay on the Gift of Tongues* (1752), "Christianisme." Naves and Christ also disclose borrowings from other authors and a comprehensive study of sources would probably reveal a great volume and diversity of influences. However, Waterman, Torrey, Wade, Crist and Naves agree: whenever Voltaire did not indicate that he was quoting, his style in the *Portatif* remains his own. His attribution of certain articles to others complemented his acknowledgement of several as his own, because he appeared to be offering two kinds of evidence in support of each other. On one hand, recognition of some articles as his own conveyed an impression of good faith. But since they had been printed without his permission, he was

---

[84] Best. 11339 to the comte d'Argental on November 5.

[85] This maneuver was nothing new. On 23 December 1760 he had written Francesco Capacelli: "Si ... une société de jeunes gens s'amusa, il y a trente ans, à faire une ... *Pucelle*; si je fus admis dans cette société; si j'eus peut-être la complaisance de me prêter à ce badinage, en y insérant les choses honnêtes et pudiques qu'on trouve par-ci par là dans ce rare ouvrage dont il ne me souvient plus du tout, je ne réponds en aucune façon d'aucune *Pucelle*" (Best. 8722). But he was fully responsible for all that was not *honnête et pudique* as well!

[86] *Romanic Review*, XXXIII, 236—249.

innocent! On the other hand, he attributed some of the more provocative articles to writers who had little to fear. Middleton was dead; Warburton, Abauzit and Polier were protestants not living in France. This diversification of authorship must have had an effect similar to multiplying places of publication. Punishing several writers in several different countries would have been difficult if not impossible.

Another writer to whom Voltaire attributed the *Portatif* is Debu, des Buttes, Desbuttes or Dubut, depending on the letter to which one refers. He first mentioned him in one to Damilaville on July 9: "Frère Cramer vous a dit qu'il y avait un vieux pédant, entouré de vieux in folios qui travaillait de tout son coeur à un ouvrage fort honnête; frère Cramer a raison" (Best. 11140). Except for the adjective *pédant*, a joke, the description applied to Voltaire himself and the *ouvrage* was certainly the second edition of the *Portatif*. On October 1 he named his alter ego "Dubut" in a letter to d'Alembert, then promptly admitted that "[il] n'a jamais existé" (Best.11276). One wonders why he told d'Alembert this "secret" and witheld it from the d'Argentals whom he wrote on the same day. In his letter to these equally good friends he associated Dubut with another "disciple": "L'auteur [du *Portatif*] est proche parent de l'ex-jésuite ... il lui a dit qu'il s'allait mettre à travailler, tout malade qu'il est. Cet auteur s'appelle Dubu, mais il a encore un autre nom; il a étudié en théologie" (Best. 11277). The "ex-Jesuit", author of the *Triumvirat* (1764), was Voltaire himself [87], who had attended a Jesuit school as a boy. Dubu's other name was likewise Voltaire, who was studying theology for the *Portatif* and suffering from little worse than hypochondria. In a letter to Damilaville that same day, Dubu became a "petit apprentif théologien de Hollande" (Best. 11278), and therefore differentiated himself from Voltaire by his country if not his interest in theology. Voltaire maintained his triple identity in another letter to the d'Argentals on October 3, asking these *divins anges* to spread their wings over "deux hommes assez singuliers; c'est le petit exjésuite en vers, et le petit huguenot des Buttes en prose" (Best. 11281). Voltaire of course wrote his tragedy in verse and his dictionary in prose. But one must evoke his stay in Geneva and his interest in sacred studies to explain the less pertinent allusion to a Huguenot.

---

[87] Voltaire announced the character to Damilaville as follows: "On a lu une esquisse [du *Triumvirat*] à nos seigneurs les comédiens, on leur a fait acroire que l'autheur était un jeune pauvre diable d'exjesuite, dont il fallait encourager le talent naissant" (Best. 11056 to Chauvelin on May 28). The Society of Jesus had been disbanded in France in 1762.

Des Buttes, he says, "m'aporta hier un gros cayer d'articles nouvaux et d'anciens articles corrigez ... C'est un travailleur qui ne laisse pas d'avoir quelque érudition orientale et qui cependant a quelquefois dans l'esprit une plaisanterie qui ressemble à celle de votre pays" (Best. 11281). This thick notebook was the manuscript of the revised edition soon to be published by Rey in Amsterdam. Des Buttes' prompt revision of the *Portatif,* his oriental erudition and his French wit all identify him as Voltaire, who seems rather pleased with himself here [88].

In a letter to Damilaville on the same day, however, Des Buttes abruptly loses his resemblance to his creator: "Je crois vous avoir mandé ... que le jeune homme nommé Des Buttes, auteur du dictionaire portatif, s'en était déclaré publiquement l'auteur" (Best. 11283). Since Besterman has discovered no such letter, Voltaire's "belief" that he had already told Damilaville about Des Buttes' public declaration may have been an attempt to pass the information off as an accepted fact. In any case Des Buttes had drunk at the Fountain of Youth. The effect had worn off by October 16 when Voltaire wrote Mme. d'Epinay: "Mr Dubut ou Des buttes, car je ne sais pas précisément son nom ... est bien vieux" (Best. 11355). This fluctuation announced the demise of the mysterious M. Desbuttes, who disappeared from the *Correspondence* after the letter to Mme. d'Epinay. Although this hoax may have caused a few useful rumors, its main purpose was assuredly to provide the *vieil acteur* with a comic role to entertain himself and his friends.

Was the rest of the campaign to disavow the *Portatif* likewise a mere role he was playing? He was certainly accustomed to such a role: "L'auteur du *Dictionnaire philosophique* a renié presque toutes ses oeuvres, à l'exception de ses pièces de théâtre et grands ouvrages historiques" [89]. He surely intended to amplify by his denials the publicity arising from the appearance of a provocative work. But did the scandal over the *Portatif* remain within the limits of his calculations? [90] A scandal there definitely was: "La tempête gronde

---

[88] "Voicy des Buttes qui entre chez moy," he exlaimed a few paragraphs later. "Il ne me donne aucun repos."

[89] Bernard Gagnebin, "la Diffusion clandestine des oeuvres de Voltaire" in *Actes du cinquième Congrès national de la Société française de littérature comparée* (Lyon, 1962), p. 129.

[90] Vercruysse entitled a chapter of his *Voltaire et Marc Michel Rey* "un Scandale calculé: le *Dictionnaire philosophique* et l'*Evangile de la Raison* (1764)", *SVEC,* LVIII, 1717—1731.

de tous côtés contre le portatif" [91]. And there are symptoms of vacillation, even fear in his correspondence. On October 29, for instance, he wrote the comte d'Argental: "J'ai pris trop d'alarmes sur ce livre" (Best. 11331) and on November 2 he told Damilaville: "Je ne me suis pas allarmé mal à propos sur ce portatif ... Il a été nécessaire de prendre à la cour des précautions qui ont coûté beaucoup à ma philosophie" (Best. 11336). These embarrassing "precautions" probably consisted in sending a sly letter disavowing the dictionary to the président Hénault (See above, p. 40), whom Louis XV had just asked to examine the work. Hénault apparently obliged Voltaire by combatting the king's suspicions of him, but Voltaire was obviously not proud of this ally [92]. Louis' unexpected intervention [93] seems to have scared him into writing Hénault.

How serious did he consider the danger when he mastered this fear? A letter from Choiseul to him on October 27 is instructive:

> Pourquoi diable vous démenez vous, Suisse marmotte, comme si vous étiez dans un bénitier? On ne vous dit mot, et certainement l'on ne veut vous faire aucun mal; vous désavouez le livre sans que l'on vous en parle, à la bonne heure; mais vous ne me persuaderez jamais qu'il n'est pas de vous; le silence sur cet ouvrage était très prudent; vos lettres multipliées sont une preuve de plus qu'il est de vous et que vous avez peur. Soyez tranquille ... regardez moi comme le serviteur de la marmotte. [94]   (Best. 11329)

Looking down from his lofty office, the minister assumed that Voltaire was writing so many letters merely to defend himself against imaginary dangers. If he would only behave himself, no harm would come to him, for Choiseul could control the situation. Voltaire quoted Choiseul, inaccurately as usual, in his letter to the comtesse d'Argental in early November: "*Vieux Suisse, vieille marmotte, vous vous agitez comme si vous étiez dans un bénitier et vous vous tourmentez pour*

---

[91] Best. 11278 from Voltaire to Damilaville on October 1.

[92] "La chose a été jusqu'au roi qu'il fallait détromper", he told the comtesse d'Argental in early November, "et vous n'imagineriez jamais de qui je me suis servi pour lui faire connaître la vérité" (Best. 11341).

[93] According to Voltaire the abbé d'Estrées had denounced him to the Bishop of Orleans and the Attorney General as the author of the *Portatif*. The presumptuous abbé harbored a secret grudge because Voltaire, technically his vassal, had failed to pay him hommage.

[94] Although Choiseul's complimentary close is a standard formula for the period, he seems to have given it its literal meaning here. He was in fact of great service to Voltaire.

bien peu de chose. Je ne suis pas tout à fait de son avis" (Best. 11341). Perhaps he did not agree because he suspected that Choiseul would protect him only as long as no political risk was involved. The deluge of letters continued to fall on Paris. Not that Voltaire was so foolish as to spurn Choiseul's protection, or that of his cousin the duc de Praslin, another friendly minister [95], not to mention Hénault. On November 7 he assured Damilaville that "il a fallu toute la protection que j'ai à la cour pour affaiblir seulement un peu l'opinion où était le roi que j'étais l'auteur du portatif" (Best. 11344). Thus his friends at court had so much influence that they could persuade the king himself, for the moment at least, to accept as false what he knew to be true.

Almost everyone, therefore, friends and enemies alike, were convinced that Voltaire had written the *Portatif*. Voltaire himself must have realized that his claims to the contrary were falling on deaf ears and only serving to maintain a convenient hypocrisy. His letter to the Academy as well as his memoir denying authorship amounted to a public repudiation of the work and that was a humiliation we know he wished to avoid. Even though he was following his own rule in sacrificing the book for the safety of the author, the necessity to do so publicly shows that he found himself in serious trouble. But the danger was not of the kind one would expect, as a letter to Damilaville on November 23 reveals: "On . . . avait parlé [du *Portatif*] au Roi en termes très forts . . . Je me trouvais précisément alors dans des circonstances très épineuses, j'y suis encor; il s'agit d'obtenir de nouvelles Lettres patentes du Roi, en faveur de la terre de Ferney. Vous m'avouerez que le portatif n'était pas une bonne recommandation. Il eût été inutile de le désavouer à la cour si je n'avais pas fait le même désaveu à la ville" (Best. 11365). He needed the letters patent to confirm his niece's right, as titular owner of Ferney, not to pay tithes to the local priest, who had initiated a lawsuit to recover them. Failure to guarantee this right, which had already been assured by previous letters patent, royal decrees and international treaties [96], would have cost a considerable sum and reduced the productivity of the estate, thus jeopardizing his security. Worse, the risk of losing a lawsuit to the "infamous" must have haunted him. For once the king of France had the means to keep him in check.

---

[95] "Mr le Duc de Praslin qui connait parfaittement mon innocence, a assuré le Roy que je n'étais point l'auteur de ce pieux ouvrage", he wrote Richelieu on 27 February 1765 (Best. 11577).

[96] Under the Old Regime one could apparently reopen any case.

In his letter to Damilaville Voltaire was probably trying to justify an act that might have seemed cowardly to this militant "philosopher". He therefore added flimsy excuses in hopes of reinforcing a solid one: "Il valait certainement mieux aller au devant de la Calomnie que d'attendre pour la réfuter quelque avanture du grand Escalier. Ne doutez pas que quelque bigot n'eût proposé mon exclusion de l'académie" (Best. 11365). As the last sentence implies, he knew of no proposals to exclude him from the Academy, which, in fact had just admitted Marmontel ,a fellow "pilosopher". Repudiation of a subversive book, moreover, would certainly not save the book itself from burning at the foot of the big staircase to the Palais de Justice in Paris, a ceremony that did not impress him anyway. Just two days before writing Damilaville he had buried the following sentences in a paragraph full of other news: "Il seroit possible qu'à la rentrée du parlement on brûlât le portatif. Il est assés bon pour mériter ce traitement" [97]. This nonchalance continued in another letter to Damilaville a week later.

Since practically no one doubted that he had authored the *Portatif*, however, the veil of "innocence" in which he had been cloaking himself was dangerously transparent. If for any reason his powerful friends had relaxed their vigilance, forthcoming retaliation against the book could have led to persecution of the author. He may have heard of the expedition undertaken that Fall by d'Hémery, *inspecteur de la librairie*: "[Il] fut envoyé à Bouillon ... dans le duché de Luxembourg, lieu de franchise sous la souveraineté du prince de Turenne. Il était accompagné d'une compagnie ... de grenadiers ... Il trouva chez Trousseau [imprimeur] ... quantité d'exemplaires de la *Tolérance*, du *Dictionnaire philosophique*, et *la Pucelle* et de beaucoup d'autres livres prohibés" [98]. As a fief Ferney was certainly less secure from such an intervention than Bouillon, despite Voltaire's bluster in 1763: "Je n'habite point en France" (Best. 10462). If the government could cross feudal borders to seize the book, it could do the same to arrest the author. Sufficiently provoked, it could goad itself into action, even high-handed action, and the Calas affair had demonstrated the arbitrary and subjective nature of what could be accepted as proof under the Old Regime. Voltaire could of course flee to Geneva, but the author of the *Portatif* would be an embarrassing if not unwelcome guest there. At his age exile was a bleak

---

[97] Best. 11362 to the comte d'Argental.
[98] Belin, *Commerce*, p. 42.

prospect and life without a country, as the younger Rousseau was learning, promised nothing but misery.

Consequently Voltaire must have understood that the danger to his person was merely less apparent than the danger to his fortune. Nevertheless, the self-confidence of 1763 subsided only on occasion in the Fall of 1764 and continued unabated in 1765. He did not hesitate to provoke a scandal even more perilous than the previous ones because he was confident in his ability to wriggle out of any predicament and survive. Contrary to critical tradition, however, it seems unlikely that his letter-writing campaign protected him more than it exposed him. Choiseul's letter demonstrates why nothing happened to the author of an impudently subversive work who insisted on broadcasting his desire to remain anonymous. Such advertising did incite public curiosity and lead to ever wider dissemination of the book, especially when the second edition began to arrive from Holland. But one must not forget that Voltaire was enjoying himself too. All the ingenious ways he found to deny his authorship only illustrated his skills as an author and he revelled in the glory of being the most famous non-author in Europe. His character was in sum so complex that playfulness, vanity and fear motivated his campaign as much as calculation.

Relief or disappointment, perhaps both, further complicated the situation by December 19 when he wrote the d'Argentals: "Je soupçonne le portatif d'avoir été noyé dans les flots d'édits portés en parlement; et quand on voudra le mettre en lumière, après l'aventure des édits, ce ne sera que du réchauffé" (Best. 11404). If indeed the affair had been buried in the dossiers awaiting the attention of Parlement, the scandal was certainly waning in Paris. But a letter to the comte d'Argental four days later shows that the mood in Geneva was downright benign: "Un magistrat vint me demander poliment la permission de brûler un certain portatif. Je lui dis que ses confrères étaient bien les maîtres pourvu qu'ils ne brûlassent pas ma personne" (Best. 11411).

Having learned, however, that the work had already been burned in The Hague, he changed his tone: "Voilà une bombe à laquelle on ne s'attendait pas ... J'ai grandpeur qu'Omer ne se réveille au bruit de la bombe" [99]. Omer Joly de Fleury was the Attorney General to whom the abbé d'Estrées had denounced the author of the *Portatif*. Having indicted *De l'Esprit* and the *Encyclopédie* in 1759, he was

---

[99] Best. 11423 to Damilaville on December 26.

now preparing an indictment which had been worrying Voltaire for some time. "Omer travaille à un réquisitoire pour le dictionaire philosophique", he told Damilaville on December 31. "Je crois que mon neveu qui est conseiller au parlement, l'empêchera de me désigner" (Best. 11433). Dompierre d'Hornoy may have succeeded in obliging his uncle, for the eventual condemnation of the *Portatif* by Parlement did not mention Voltaire.

Once he had brought the situation in Paris under control, he deemed it necessary to vindicate himself in Geneva again. On 12 January 1765 he wrote the Petit Conseil: "Parmi les libelles pernicieux dont cette ville est inondée depuis quelque temps, tous imprimés à Amsterdam chez Marc Michel Rey, il arrive Lundi prochain chez le nommé Chirol, Libraire de Genève, un ballot contenant des Dictionnaires philosophique [et d'autres ouvrages]" (Best. 11471). At first glance this letter seems a spineless betrayal of a bookseller who was risking his livelihood to disseminate Voltaire's works. When interrogated, though, Chirol declared that he had ordered the shipment intercepted and returned to Amsterdam. This incident, which cleared Voltaire in Geneva without harming anyone, was too slick not to have been arranged. I suspect that he rewarded Chirol [100] for his troubles. His letter to the Petit Conseil seems to have terminated his letter-writing campaign, for afterwards the *Portatif* received considerably less attention in his correspondence.

As we have seen, this campaign had not prevented him from preparing a second edition. On 3 October 1765 he had written the d'Argentals that des Buttes: "m'aporta hier un gros cayer d'articles nouveaux et d'anciens articles corrigez ... Je les ay trouvez ... plus circomspects et plus intéressants que les anciens" (Best. 11281). The manuscript of the second edition, which Voltaire considered more interesting and less provocative than the first, was ready. On October 7 a letter to Henri Rieu, who was handling his business with Rey, suggests that he had forwarded the manuscript even before writing the d'Argentals: "[Mr De Rieu] est prié de vouloir bien dire si Michel Rey a reçu le paquet ... Il doit y avoir des frais assez considérables pour l'affranchissement de ces paquets" (Best. 11289). The considerable shipping charge indicates that *le paquet* in question was no letter, but rather a package. Frequent allusions in Voltaire's correspondence over the next few weeks to an improved and expanded edition of the

---

[100] Best. 11844 (undated) shows that he did business with Chirol: "Je prie instamment monsieur Cramer, de faire envoyer par Chirol ces deux volumes [unnamed] qu'on a imprimés sous mon nom".

dictionary show that it contained des Buttes' *gros cayer*. Rey had finished printing the work by November 29, since he shipped copies of it to two booksellers on that date [101]. On December 11 Voltaire announced the new edition to Damilaville: "Le Portatif est d'une société de gens de Lettres; c'est sous ce titre qu'il vient d'être imprimé en Hollande" (Best. 11396). He continued the habitual claim of collective authorship in another letter to the d'Argentals on December 19 and added: "On l'a imprimé en Hollande ... il s'en est débité quatre mille en huit jours" (Best. 11404). If Voltaire was not exaggerating, Rey had therefore printed a great many more copies than Cramer. The addition of seven new articles and a supplementary section to the work as well as the publicity Voltaire was giving the rare first edition justified Rey's expectations of sales success.

In 1765 at least three more editions [102] reproduced the text of Rey's publication and in the Fall of that year Varberg in Amsterdam printed a revised version including sixteen new articles, two supplementary sections, sixteen additions to existing articles and a revised version of "Salomon". The Varberg edition had appeared by October 16 when Voltaire sent Mme. du Deffand a copy and gloated to d'Alembert that the *Portatif* had gone through six editions in eighteen months. Earlier, on May 27, he "complained" to Damilaville that the author of an English imitation had stolen more than twenty "chapters" from the work "que l'ignorance et la calomnie m'ont si grossièrement imputé, et pour comble de bêtise, il y a dans d'autres chapitres des phrases entières de moi mot pour mot. Je me mettrais dans une belle colère si l'âge et les maladies n'affaiblissaient les passions" (Best. 11767). Age and his alleged bad health had certainly not hurt his sense of humor. In reality the extraordinary success of his book was not conducive to tantrums, authentic or otherwise. Condemning it to a public burning by the executioner in Paris, Geneva, Bern and the Hague as well as placing it on the Index in the Vatican during 1764—1765 seems merely to have spread the sort of intellectual epidemic that one generally associates with more recent literary history.

In a letter to Helvétius on 25 June 1765, Voltaire made a serious assessment of progress in the war on the "infamous", which he had implied his book would virtually "crush": "Je sais bien qu'on ne

---

[101] "Le 29, Rey expédiait 10 exemplaires à Staatman, et 12 autres à Janssen, deux libraires de La Haye." Vercruysse, *Voltaire et Marc Michel Rey*, p. 1718.

[102] On April 24 he wrote Damilaville: "La bonne cause triomphe. Nouvelle édition du portatif en Hollande, à Berlin, à Londres" (Best. 11719). The tactic is familiar. The title pages of all three editions displays the usual "Londres".

détruira pas La hiérarchie établie ... On n'abolira pas la secte dominante; mais certainement on la rendra moins dominante et moins dangereuse. Le christianisme deviendra plus raisonnable et par conséquent moins persécuteur" (Best. 11808). By his own admission, therefore, he had not been able to "porter les derniers coups à l'infâme" (Best. 11058) as he had told Damilaville shortly before publication of the *Portatif*. His less exuberant prediction in the letter to Helvétius is realistic for the long term, but optimistic for the short. There can be no question that he had struck a powerful blow and that increasing numbers of his contemporaries would deserve the title "philosophers". But pious reaction to the progress of "philosophy" would continue to produce setbacks, some of which would be quite discouraging.

In the meantime, however, the remaining ten volumes of the *Encyclopédie* appeared, thanks to the "tolerance" of Malesherbes, Directeur de la Librairie. Volume VIII contained Voltaire's "Idole" and volume X, Polier's "Messie". Voltaire had received his copy of the work by 4 February 1766, as he informed Damilaville: "Il est arrivé, il est arrivé ... On relie jour et nuit [103]. Je grille d'impatience" (Best. 12285). There is no reason to suspect this enthusiasm, since in his correspondence he soon began to comment on the articles he was reading. In a letter to d'Alembert on April 5 he deplored that Parisian subscribers had not yet received their copies. What could the authorities possibly fear, he slyly argued, from a twenty-volume work priced at a hundred *écus*? Such a work would never provoke a revolution: "Ce sont les petits livres portatifs à trente sous qui sont à craindre. Si l'évangile avait coûté douze cents sesterces, jamais la religion chrétienne ne se serait établie" [104] (Best. 12362). As usual he was pleading the cause of his dictionary at the expense of the Encyclopedia, but this time on the pretext of sympathy for his friendly rivals in Paris. To the advantage of size enjoyed by the *Portatif* he now added that of cost, an even more important consideration and one that certainly must have contributed to its popularity.

As the book continued to sell, the threat of reprisal appeared to subside. Judging from past experience in subversive publication, Voltaire could reasonably expect no further trouble. Nevertheless, a disaster finally occurred on 1 July 1766, when the twenty-one year old chevalier de La Barre was put to the Question, beheaded and

---

[103] The work had been shipped unbound.

[104] Further evidence that Voltaire considered "philosophy" a new kind of religion.

burned in the market place of Abbeville along with a copy of the *Portatif*.

One must distinguish between Voltaire's knowledge of the case and the facts, most of which Marc Chassaigne [105] has gleaned from the available documents. A poorly educated orphan, La Barre and his older brother were the survivors of a decaying branch of a prominent noble family. His mundane cousin the abbess of the Willancourt convent in Abbeville, took him in after the death of his father and provided for him. But parental neglect and his own mediocre intelligence had already aggravated an adolescent obsession with sex and revolt against religion. In Abbeville he made friends with other youths who resembled him and began to admire the older, more daring Gaillard d'Etallonde, the son of a local magistrate. One night d'Etallonde mutilated a wooden crucifix venerated by the townspeople, thus provoking a great scandal. Meanwhile, La Barre had attracted less attention by defecating on the pedestal of a stone cross in a churchyard. Neither culprit was immediately identified.

Duval de Soicourt, the *mayeur* of Abbeville, took charge of the cases and persuaded the aging bishop of Amiens to conduct an amende honorable that greatly impressed the populace. He also persuaded the local priests to fulminate a series of monitories in order to scare all possible witnesses into testifying. Although most of the evidence that accumulated was hearsay, it implicated d'Etallonde, La Barre and their younger companion Moisnel in a number of sacrilegious acts, all of them trivial in comparison to the mutilation of the crucifix. The worst was their failure to remove their caps in the rain as they hurried across the path of an approaching religious procession bearing the Blessed Sacrament. Among the charges to which La Barre confessed was his habit of genuflecting before a "tabernacle" in his room consisting of a bookshelf. Among other volumes, most of them pornography, the *Portatif* enjoyed this dubious honor.

Why did the magistrate Belleval, once a frequent guest in the abbess' salon, persuade a number of people to testify against La Barre? Chassaigne argues that he was jealous because she had transferred her attentions from him to the young man. Meanwhile, Duval was neglecting the mutilation of the crucifix, probably to avoid trouble with d'Etallonde's family, and concentrating on the other

---

[105] *Procès du chevalier de La Barre* (Paris 1920). See also Edouard Hertz, *Voltaire und die Strafrechtspflege* (Stuttgart, 1887), pp. 243—274.

offenses. When finally he ordered the three young men arrested, La Barre and Moisnel were taken while d'Etallonde was nowhere to be found. Belleval, who happened to be Moisnel's guardian, then scared the boy into betraying La Barre. But Moisnel exposed others as well, including d'Etallonde and Belleval's own son.

Belleval then went over to the other side, joining the abbess and her friend Douville, a former *mayeur,* who was trying to help her defend La Barre. With his assistance she drafted a letter to her cousin the président d'Ormesson of the Paris Parlement, whom she persuaded to appeal to the Attorney General Joly de Fleury. Joly also received a letter from Hecquet the Abbeville prosecutor who asked for instructions, probably expecting him to recommend the usual leniency in cases involving noblemen. When the Attorney General finally saw fit to answer, his recommendation was quite different: "Je ne crois pas que vous puissiez vous dispenser de suivre l'instruction dans toute la rigueur de l'ord [onnance]" [106].

A last-minute retraction by Moisnel of all that he had said against his co-defendants did not stop Hecquet from recommending the galleys for La Barre, or Duval, from sentencing him to death. Yet neither explicitly attributed the mutilation of the crucifix to him. While Hecquet proposed to burn all the pornographic and sacrilegious books found in his possession, Duval singled out the *Portatif.* Joly, who was no friend of Voltaire, may have encouraged him to take this step [107]. Duval's severity flattered the mood of the Paris Parlement and Louis XV, who were competing with each other to repair their reputations as defenders of the Faith after banishing the Jesuits in 1764. When the lawyer Linguet and seven of his colleagues published a memoir in support of La Barre, it was immediately sup-

---

[106] Quoted from Chassaigne, *Procès,* p. 118: Bibliothèque Nationale, fonds Joly de Fleury, f°45. Joly did not specify which ordonnance, but that was apparently not necessary under the Old Regime. Nevertheless, Voltaire and Gaston Marchou both refer to an ordinance promulgated by Louis XIV against the Huguenots in 1681. See Marchou's "Le Chevalier de La Barre et la raison d'état," *Revue de Paris,* LXXII (juillet-août 1965), p. 116. On 25 July 1766 Voltaire asked Elie de Beaumont "s'il est vrai qu'il y ait une loy de 1681 par laquelle on puisse condamner à la mort ceux qui sont coupables de quelques indécences impies" (Best. 12566).

[107] Chaissaigne suspects that compromising documents were removed from the archives concerning the case. The least one can say of Joly is that he was a hypocrite. In 1744 he had written Feydeau de Marville, the lieutenant de police of Paris, asking for a copy of Voltaire's complete works which had recently been seized. "Je fais assez de cas de ces ouvrages saisis" (Best. 2815), he explained.

pressed. The Grand' Chambre of Parlement had to review the Abbeville decision, but there the conseiller Pasquier, another enemy of Voltaire, stampeded the judges into confirming it. The king could still commute La Barre's sentence and the bishop of Amiens, an unexpected ally, pleaded his case at court. But his Majesty had kneeled in public before the same kind of procession that La Barre and his friends had ignored. Anxious to save his soul and obtain additional funds from Parlement, he refused to act. In Abbeville La Barre's composure in the face of torture and death was interpreted as the impudence of Christ's murderer.

Chassaigne and Marchou try to acquit the Church and convict the State of this atrocity, but both institutions are clearly responsible. Even though the Church did not deliberately seek to inflame the populace, it fostered a climate of superstition and fanaticism that made pranks seem like crimes. As for the State, it murdered a convenient scapegoat in hopes of enforcing a religious discipline it considered vital to social order. Incompatible with free thought, the two institutions found themselves united in an attempt to eradicate a threat to their existence. Unlike the previous burnings of the *Portatif*, this one was not intended merely to discourage dissemination of the work, but rather to avenge the affront of its publication.

> Ainsi la même flamme consumerait dans ses replis le maître et le disciple. Qui donc douterait, en les voyant ensemble hissés sur le bûcher, que le chevalier n'eût été conduit au supplice par le livre séducteur? C'était un coup de maître, condamner Voltaire nommément désigné dans son oeuvre antichrétienne, le dénoncer comme pervertisseur de la jeunesse, un assassin des âmes. Quelle physionomie nouvelle, vraiment imprévue pendant toute l'information, ce choix arbitraire, mais si judicieux, du livre philosophique imprimait à la chétive affaire des polissons d'Abbeville! Eux, se mettant tous ensemble, eussent été bien empêchés d'assembler une idée, les voilà métamorphosés en suppôts dangereux de doctrines subversives. Leur cause, ainsi amplifiée, devenait intéressante, digne enfin d'occuper l'attention et de susciter l'éloquence vengeresse de M. M. du Parlement. Car c'était la philosophie nouvelle maintenant qui se trouverait l'accusée véritable.
>
> (Chassaigne, p. 157)

When Voltaire first learned of the La Barre affair, he did not even know that "philosophy" was involved in any way, let alone the *Portatif*. On 16 June 1766 he wrote his nephew in the Paris Parlement: "Je suis très touché du sort des Polyeuctes et des Néarques que les Welches brûlent; il me semble que les petites maisons étaient le vrai partage de ces messieurs, et quant à l'homme qui s'est mis au cou un ruban, je lui aurais conseillé de le serrer pour faire une amende honorable plus complette" (Best. 12480). The last remark reflects his early assumption that the bishop of Amiens was the villian of the affair. Polyeucte [108] and Néarque are of course the Christian martyrs in Corneille's tragedy *Polyeucte* (1642) which he had commented in his 1764 edition of the great classic. Welches, on the other hand, is the name he gave the French people when he wished to express contempt for them. His sentence therefore presents a disturbing mixture of pity and wit. Obviously he had not yet understood that the defendants in the Abbeville trial were not martyrs (madmen to him), but victims. The comparison of La Barre and his companions to Corneille's heroes, however ridiculous, becomes tedious in his subsequent correspondence.

Later in the month of June he wrote Damilaville that he hoped Louis would pardon the young men [109]. By July 1, the date of La Barre's execution, he had heard that the judges were blaming the accused's errors on books by "philosophers". He immediately protested to d'Alembert, Damilaville and the marquis d'Argence. "De jeunes étourdis", he told the latter, "que la démence et la débauche ont entrainés jusqu'à des prophanations publiques, ne sont pas gens à lire des livres de philosophie" (Best. 12504). His abuse of the defendants, whom he did not know, apparently came less from anger than fear. It is true that he joined the Encyclopedists in recommending respect for religious conventions [110], which he considered useful to social order. Yet his own *Portatif* was a far more destruc-

---

[108] In the *Traité sur la Tolérance*, Voltaire wrote: "Considérons le martyre de saint Polyeucte. Le condamna-t-on pour sa religion seule? Il va dans le temple où l'on rend aux dieux des actions de grâces pour la victoire de l'empereur Décius; il y insulte les sacrificateurs, il renverse et brise les autels et les statues: quel est le pays du monde où l'on pardonnerait un tel attentat?" Moland, XXV, 48.

[109] "On m'a mandé que le parlement n'avait point signé l'arrêt qui condamne les jeunes fous d'Abbeville, et qu'il avait voulu laisser à leurs parents le temps d'obtenir du roi une commutation de peine, je souhaite que cette nouvelle soit vraie" (Best. 12491). Parlement's delay in signing is a tradition that Chassaigne has not been able to document.

[110] "Les deux insensés, dit on … ont répondu dans leurs interrogatoires qu'ils avaient puisé leur aversion pour nos saints mystères, dans les livres des encyclopédistes et de plusieurs philosophes de nos jours. Cette nouvelle est sans doute fabriquée par les ennemis de la raison, de la vertu et de la religion. Qui sait mieux que vous combien tous ces philosophes ont tâché d'inspirer le plus profond respect pour les lois reçues?" (Best. 12505 to Damilaville on July 1).

tive act of public desecration than those La Barre had committed. Perhaps he already suspected that Parlement had not forgotten.

News of La Barre's execution, which probably strengthened this suspicion, had arrived by July 7. On this day he had his secretary Wagnière write the veuve Duchêne for him on the pretext that he was "très malade" (Best. 12515). But this illness did not stop him from composing a number of other letters himself to protest the accusation that "philosophy" was responsible for the defendant's behavior. "Le conseiller Pasquier a dit en plein parlement", he wrote the abbé Morellet, "que les jeunes gens d'Abbeville [111] ... avaient puisé leur impiété ... dans les ouvrages des philosophes ... [qu'on] a fait passer pour les véritables autheurs du supplice" (Best. 12517). The realization that "they" might have lived had he persecuted the "infamous" less violently was beginnning to dawn on him. "Mon coeur est flétri", he wrote Damilaville that same day. "Je suis tenté d'aller mourir dans une terre où les hommes soient moins injustes" (Best. 12514). In another letter to his niece the marquise de Florian, who lived near Abbeville, he asked for more information. His curiosity was increasing as rapidly as his anxiety.

The most important letter he wrote that day seems to have been addressed to himself. This document accompanied his other letters in 1766 just as his *mémoire* had in 1764. Its flagrant inaccuracy appears to have resulted from misinformation and speculation.

Although the *Portatif* alone had burned with the chevalier's body, for instance, Voltaire gives a whole list of books which, according to him, shared this fate: "les pensées philosophiques, le Sopha de Crébillon, des lettres sur les miracles, le dictionnaire philosophique, deux petits volumes de Bayle, un discours de l'empereur Julien grec et français, un abrégé de l'histoire de l'église de Fleuri et l'anatomie de la messe" [112]. A short story, the *Sopha* (1742) by Crébillon fils had not been linked to the chevalier in any way, but it resembles most of the works in his possession by its sexual titillation, if not by its literary quality. La Barre admitted to kneeling in mock prayer before *Thérèse philosophe; le Canapé couleur de feu, histoire galante; la Belle Allemande [ou] les Galanteries de Thérèse* and the notorious

---

[111] At this point Voltaire believed that there were several victims.
[112] *Correspondence*, LXII, 243.

Portier des Chartreux [113]. Along with the *Belle Allemande* and the *Canapé; les Amusements des dames de B[ruxelles], histoire honnête et presque édifiante; le Cousin de Mahomet [ou] la folie salutaire* and *le Sultan Misapouf et la princesse Grisemine* [114] were found in his room at the convent. Perhaps Voltaire did not know that the chevalier also had a copy of his own famous contribution to this genre, *la Pucelle,* which was masquerading as a prayer book [115].

Most of the works Voltaire gives La Barre are "philosophical" in nature, such as the *Pensées philosophiques* [116], the *Dictionnaire philosophique, Collection des Lettres sur les miracles* (1765), also by Voltaire, and the *Défense du paganisme, par l'empereur Julien, en grec et en français* (Berlin, 1764) edited and translated by the marquis d'Argens. The two small works by Bayle may be the *Réponse d'un nouveau converti à la lettre d'un réfugié* (1689) and *Avis important aux réfugiés (1692)* [117]. Voltaire's motives for mentioning the two works by Bayle may also have been vaguely "philosophical". But the "philosophical" works which actually passed through La Barre's hands were less obscure. Helvétius' *De l'Esprit* belonged to his "tabernacle" and figured in the testimony of the trial, although the police did not find it in his room. Voltaire's own *Lettres philosophiques* (1732) and *Epître à Uranie* (1722) likewise enjoyed this doubtful status. Chassaigne suggests that d'Etallonde had lent him these three works and then taken them back before the seizure took place. Whether Voltaire knew which books La Barre had actually possessed or not, his list tended to spread the responsibility for the young man's "philosophy".

In his *Anatomie de la messe* (Genève, 1641) the calvinist Pierre du Moulin shows that "la messe est contraire à la parole de Dieu" (title-page). A two-volume *Abrégé* of Claude Fleury's *Histoire ecclésiastique* (1691—1743) in 36 volumes was published by Frederick and the

---

[113] Marquis d'Argens, *Thérèse* (La Have, 1748); Fougeret de Montbron, *le Canapé* (Amsterdam, 1714); Gervaise de La Touche, *le Portier,* first printed as *Histoire de Dom B ... portier ...* (1748). The latter went through a number of editions and figured in several seizures of illegal books.

[114] Chevrier, *les Amusements* (La Haye, 1762); Fromaget, *le Cousin* (Constantinople [Paris], 1742); abbé de Voisenon, *le Sultan* (Londres, 1746).

[115] Copies of the *Portatif* were also said to have been bound as prayer books.

[116] The work by Diderot (Paris, 1746), the collection of Voltaire texts under the same title (1766) or both?

[117] Although Bayle's authorship of the latter work has been questioned, Elisabeth Labrousse assigns it to him in her *Pierre Bayle* (La Haye, 1963).

abbé de Prades in 1766. Voltaire was in the habit of using both of these works, which were in his library, against the institutions represented by their authors. The chevalier's "tabernacle" boasted a somewhat similar work, the *Oeuvres* (1761—1764) in four volumes of Villart de Grécourt, chanoine de Tours. One wonders what it was doing there.

Among the books Voltaire says were burned with the young man's body, only the *Portatif* actually suffered this fate. But such information was probably not available to Voltaire [118] who, in his open letter, seems to have imagined what he could not find out. By placing Crébillon's story on the chevalier's bookshelf, he was no doubt trying to salvage the young man's literary taste, which as he apparently suspected was adolescently pornographic. He must have intended the "philosophical" works as evidence of an intellectual curiosity that was sadly lacking in La Barre, to whom such books appealed only because of their shocking reputation among the pious. Finally, the devout work tends to belie the charge of iconoclasm leveled against this alleged disciple of "philosophy", who was really the innocent victim of a quarrel that did not concern him. However ingenious as guesswork, this phony booklist was an error in judgement. Instead of denying his responsibility in the affair, which he had a perfect right to do, Voltaire tended to magnify it. His ill-considered attempt to introduce the *Portatif* to better company was one of many symptoms that the affair had profoundly disturbed him.

His open letter also included an anecdote that would awaken the old anger against him in Paris. In defending La Barre, he asserted: "Le cardinal Le Camus dont il était parent avait commis des prophanations bien plus grandes, car il avait communié un cochon avec une hostie. Il ne fut qu'exilé; il devint ensuite cardinal et mourut en odeur de sainteté" [119]. La Barre, on the other hand, had died a horrible death for having failed to doff his cap and other such trivia. According to the *Mémoires secrets*, three copies of the letter were circulating in Paris that summer, where they were, as usual, being attributed to Voltaire. The style, the tone and the contents of the work as described in the *Mémoires* all identify it as the document in question and this description includes the story of the cardinal who had once administered the communion to a pig. "Le parlement est

---

[118] The Calas affair reveals how secretive an Old Regime tribunal could be when under attack.

[119] *Correspondence*, XLII, 243—244.

furieux contre ces lettres, et l'on assure que le premier président en a porté des plaintes au roi" (III, 61). Although Wagnière does not corroborate this development, Voltaire was apparently running the same risk as in 1764, for he would soon resort to the usual precaution of fugitives from *lettres de cachet*.

By July 12 he knew the worst, "la funeste catastrophe dont on veut me rendre en quelque façon responsable", as he described it to Damilaville. "Vous savez que je n'ai aucune part au livre que ces pauvres insensés adoraient à genoux" (Best. 12525). One wonders why the usually skeptical Voltaire took this accusation seriously. Did the shock of finding himself directly implicated in the affair numb his rapid reflexes? At the head of his next letter to Damilaville, written a day or two later, one reads: "Aux eaux de Rolle, en Suisse" (Best 12529). It would be naïve to assume that his sudden departure from Ferney was merely to improve his health. Had he not already confided in Damilaville that he was tempted to go and die in a country where men were less unjust? He devoted his entire letter from Rolle to the La Barre case and included a *relation* of the affair, or a copy of his open letter [120]. In a letter to the d'Argentals, which resembles many others from this period, he addressed himself to Parisians in general: "Courez du bûcher au bal, et de la grève à l'opéra comique, rouez Calas, pendez Sirven, brûlez cinq pauvres jeunes gens qu'il fallait, comme disent mes anges, mettre six mois à St Lazare. Je ne veux respirer le même air que vous" [121] (Best. 12537). When one considers that the d'Argentals (and Voltaire himself) belonged to this accursed race, one realizes how well they deserved the title "angels". In fact some of this vituperation tended to implicate these ever faithful friends in a more personal way, especially the references to a frivolous taste for spectacle. They willingly provided Voltaire with invaluable services in overseeing the production of his plays in Paris. His condemnation of Parisian society as one devoted only to its own pleasures and indifferent to acts of injustice, however true, does not seem very diplomatic, even though the d'Argentals were used to hearing it from him.

He forgot the frivolity of Parisian society in a letter to the marquis de Florian on July 28. "Je viens de lire le mémoire signé de huit

---

[120] And not his *Relation de la mort du chevalier de La Barre* (1767). The latter was written later and contained more accurate information.

[121] In this letter he also wrote: "Je vous demande en grâce de m'apprendre s'il n'y a rien de nouveau ... Je vous conjure encore une fois, de me dire tout ce que vous savez" (Best. 12537). Thus he continued to crave for information that would further horrify him.

avocats", he announced and he promptly reported all that he had learned. The memoir had informed him, in particular, of the subterfuge that had made it possible to punish La Barre for d'Étallonde's crime: "[Ni] la procédure, ni la sentence, ni l'arrêt n'ont fait aucune mention [du] crucifix ... Les enquêtes faites sur cette prophanation aiant été jointes aux autres corps du délit ont produit dans les esprits une fermentation qui n'a pas peu contribué à ... la catastrophe" (Best. 12572). Duval had combined evidence against a culprit he did not know (or did not want to recognize) with evidence against La Barre whom he had persuaded to confess. To hide this questionable procedure he had kept the crucifix out of all the official documents concerning the trial. That the chevalier had nevertheless multilated it was probably as common an assumption in Abbeville as the *Portatif*'s evil influence on him was in Paris.

"Ils en ont menti les vilains Welches ... les assassins en robe", begins a letter to Damilaville dated August 18. Voltaire had received further information from the marquise de Florian, which led him to believe that "par une insigne fourberie ... on a substitué le *Dictionnaire philosophique* au *Portier des Chartreux*" (Best. 12614). Both works were of course present in the "tabernacle". To this erroneous conclusion he added another, which I will quote from a letter to Richelieu the next day: "La Barre ... n'avait jamais eu [le Portatif] ... Et il n'y avait personne de la bande qui fût capable de lire un livre de philosophie" (Best. 12616). Though inaccurate perhaps where d'Etallonde is concerned, the second sentence certainly applies to La Barre. His poor intelligence would prove to be a source of embarassment to Voltaire in his attempts to rehabilitate the young man's memory. For the present, he was grasping at straws when he assumed that his enemies had substituted the *Portatif* for the *Portier* and that the chevalier had never possessed his book.

Though subject to momentary panic or dejection in such crises, he always rebounded with new energy and determination. He had done so in 1764 and he would do so again in 1766. In a letter to the d'Argentals on September 13 he deplored the Calas affair, the Sirven case and then, without mentioning La Barre, he went on to deny having written the *Portatif* "qui [pourtant] n'enseigne que la vertu" (Best. 12665). To forget the atrocity of Abbeville at such a time and in such a context was a sign of health. Not that the affair had completely faded from his memory, however, for on September 19 he wrote Chabanon: "Les Calas, les Sirven, les Labarre ont déchiré mon coeur; et par une fatalité singulière, je me suis trouvé engagé dans les trois aventures. La première a été réparée; je n'ai qu'une faible espérance pour la seconde; et la troisième m'afflige sans consolation" (Best. 12683). Although he had obviously regained his sense of perspective, he thus ranked the La Barre affair as the one that would continue to torment him. Led by the violent Pasquier and probably the cunning Joly, his enemies in Parlement had succeeded in exacting a cruel revenge for his having challenged them. As Gabriel Cramer wrote Johann Sinner, "Les Parlements... veulent avoir l'air de respecter la Religion, & le supplice... ou l'assassinat du Chevalier des Barres, c'est ce qu'ils appellent la venger" (Best. 12652).

But Voltaire had the last word in this dispute. Among the pieces he devoted to La Barre [122] was the article "Torture" which he added to his dictionary in 1769. Having described the case with nonchalant sarcasm, he concluded: "Ce n'est pas dans le XIIIe ou dans le XIVe siècle que cette aventure est arrivée, c'est dans le XVIIIe" (p. 410). His air of innocent simplicity must have made the remark seem all the more scathing to his contemporaries. Most of them looked upon the Middle Ages as very "dark" indeed and upon their own century as an age of enlightenment.

Among works that had inspired this belief were of course the *Portatif* and especially the *Encyclopédie*. The history of the former continued to entangle itself in that of the latter during the sixties as it had during the fifties and as the *Questions sur l'Encyclopédie* would in the seventies. In 1766 Voltaire appears to have even tried for the third time [123] to combine his alphabetical project with Diderot's in a country where he might bring the encyclopedists to greater militancy.

He may not have had this scheme in mind yet on June 21 when in a letter to Frederick the Great, which has not survived [124], he asked for permission to settle in Cleves, a Prussian territory on the Rhine

---

[122] *Relation de la mort du chevalier de La Barre* (1767); "Crimes ou délits de temps et de lieu", an article in the *Questions; le Cri du sang innocent* (1775) and "du Sacrilège" in *le Prix de la justice et de l'humanité*. The affair is the subject of much correspondence as well.

[123] Not including his support of Catherine the Great's invitation to Diderot in 1762 to move the Encyclopedia to Russia. There is no evidence that Voltaire wished to accompany it there.

[124] That Frederick explicitly answered this letter in Best. 12522 proves its existence. Since he announced his contribution to the defense of Sirven in his answer, Besterman has placed Voltaire's letter, in which the latter requested the contribution, on June 21 when he made similar requests to the Landgrave of Hesse-Cassel and the Duchess of Saxe-Gotha.

near Holland [125]. "Je vois avec étonnement par votre lettre", answered Frederick in early July, "que vous pourriez choisir une autre retraite que la Suisse & que vous pensez au pays de Clèves. Cet asile vous sera ouvert en tout temps. Comment le refuserais je à un homme qui a tant fait d'honneur aux lettres, à sa patrie, à l'humanité, enfin à son siècle" (Best. 12522). Frederick then assured Voltaire of the ease with which he could make the trip, "sans presque sortir de votre lit". Surprised especially by his own luck, he was therefore as anxious in 1766 to lure him back as he had been in 1753 to keep him from leaving. Since he mentioned Voltaire alone, however, there is no reason to assume that the latter had already proposed to move the Encyclopedia to Cleves.

The burning of the *Portatif* with La Barre's head and body appears to have reawakened this idea. When Voltaire wrote Damilaville on July 7, the day he learned of this atrocity, that he was tempted to go and die in a country where men were less unjust, his intentions were certainly not limited to Rolle. On July 21 he sent Damilaville another letter from this spa, expressing his determination not to be overcome by grief and anger, but rather to find a healthier retreat: "Je prendrai probablement le parti d'aller finir mes jours dans un pays où je pourrai faire du bien. Je ne serai pas le seul. Il se peut faire que le règne de la raison et de la vraie religion s'établisse bientôt" (Best. 12551). "Le prince qui favorisera cette entreprise", he added, would welcome Damilaville. "J'ai commencé déjà à prendre des mesures" (Best. 12551). The last sentence reconfirms the existence of his original letter to Frederick, whose consent he seems to have received. Although the nature of the enterprise remained vague, it would be collective and perhaps inaugurate the rule of "philosophy", "the true faith". Voltaire would participate in the venture.

Two days later he wrote Diderot, exhorting him to leave "le pays où vous avez le malheur de vivre" for one "où vous auriez la liberté entière... d'imprimer... Vous auriez des compagnons et des disciples... Enfin vous quitteriez l'esclavage pour la liberté" (Best.

---

[125] Frederick's lieutenant, earl marshal Keith, who informed Jean-Jacques Rousseau of this request from Postdam on July 3, attributed the following motive to Voltaire: "La représentation de plusieurs évêques au roi de France, contre plusieurs qui ont écrit contre la religion établie. Voltaire en a pris vivement l'alarme" (*Correspondance de Rousseau*, ed. Dufour, XV, 290). This letter also reveals that Keith shared Rousseau's hostility to Voltaire.. The latter's correspondence presents no evidence of alarm due to complaints by bishops. Keith was probably thinking of the controversy over the *Portatif* two years earlier.

12559). The rest of the letter is equally persuasive. What Voltaire expected Diderot to do in Cleves does not come into question, but which of the two would decide how it would be done? Would Diderot be Voltaire's "companion" or his "disciple"? While both were experienced encyclopedists, each had his own opinion of what an alphabetical work should accomplish, as demonstrated by the contrast between the *Encyclopédie* and the *Portatif*. Nowhere in his correspondence from this period did Voltaire deal with this problem.

He made the same invitation to d'Alembert that day and enclosed his *relation* of the La Barre affair, asking him to "l'envoyer à frère Frédéric, afin qu'il accorde une protection plus marquée et plus durable à cinq ou six hommes de mérite qui veulent [cultiver en paix la raison] dans une province méridionale de ses états" (Best. 12557). Since Cleves is by no means in the South, one can only assume that he intended to confuse the French police who had been opening his mail. His language suggests that he had already sent Frederick a second letter proposing to settle a modest group of encyclopedists on his territory, in his château Moyland where they had first met in 1740.

In two more days he composed still another letter to Damilaville in which he renewed his invitation to the latter and lavished encouragements on the Encyclopedists. "[A Cleves] on ... établirait une imprimerie ... [et] une autre manufacture plus importante ... celle de la vérité" (Best. 12565). Presumably he would offer the same financial backing as in 1758. This time, however, he was proposing to found not just a factory, but a complete industry for the production of "philosophy". Perhaps he would have asked Cramer to supervise printing and Diderot, research, while he himself would naturally assume the presidency of the company.

In any event the latest version of his dream is not entirely fantastic. In all of his letters to the Encyclopedists he cultivated their disgust for the La Barre affair, no doubt in order to jarr them loose from their Parisian servitude. Since Diderot had finally managed to publish the rest of the *Encyclopédie*, he and his collaborators had no further obligations to the publishers who had provided financial backing for the project. They were free to leave if they wished and to do as they pleased. On the other hand, nearly twenty years of persecution in one form or another was no incentive to stay. A letter from Damilaville to Voltaire on July 31 revealed that they were taking the proposition more seriously than the previous ones: "Platon ... va venir ... conférer avec moi plus particulièrement que nous n'avons pu le faire encore sur l'affaire en question. J'en ai beaucoup

causé hier avec Protagoras [d'Alembert]. Personne ne dit non ...
Platon pense bien comme vous sur la révolution que cela pourrait
produire, et il est sûr que rien ne serait plus capable d'accélerer les
progrès du bien" (Best. 12579). One can only speculate on the joy
this letter occasioned when it arrived at Ferney, for Voltaire had
arranged for Damilaville to correspond with a cautious and laconic
individual named Boursier, whom he had invented to foil the police.
The latter's reaction to Damilaville's letter is nevertheless intriguing:
"Je crains bien que ce ne soit un beau roman" (Best. 12598; Aug. 9).

Whatever confidence Voltaire may have had in his chances of success, he spared no effort in pursuing his dream. Another letter for
Damilaville left Ferney on August 4 with more of the same enticing
language, but towards the end Boursier forgot himself and mentioned
"le projet de réduire [le *Dictionnaire des sciences et des arts*] et de
l'imprimer en pays étranger" (Best. 12584). Voltaire's constant ob-
jection to the *Encyclopédie* was its prolixity and its benignity, weaknesses that he had boasted of overcoming in the *Portatif*. To him
"reducing" the Encyclopedia obviously meant fashioning it into a
"philosophical" weapon like his own dictionary. Thus the first time
he had been specific about his intentions in promoting the Cleves
project he had given himself away. His remark may have dampened
any enthusiasm the respectful, but not very docile Diderot had for
the proposal.

A few days later Frederick granted his second request, which has
also disappeared: "Vous me parlez d'une colonie de philosophes qui
se proposent de s'établir à Clèves. Je ne m'y oppose point ... à con-
dition qu'ils ménagent ceux qui doivent être ménagés, et ... [qu'ils]
observent de la décence dans leurs écrits" (Best. 12594). Admittedly
he does not sound very enthusiastic, but he would reiterate his approval in less than a week and, as Naves points out, "[il] savait fort
bien refuser" [126]. Convinced that Frederick would cooperate, Voltaire
spent the rest of the month pressing the Encyclopedists for an answer.
In a letter to Damilaville on August 31 he even invited Diderot to
come and negociate with him at Ferney. All to no avail [127].

Diderot finally answered in early October. His letter, a minor
masterwork in its own right, begins with a full page of sentences
introduced by the phrase "Je sçais bien que ..." (Best. 12719). In

---

[126] *Voltaire et l'Encyclopédie*, p. 94.

[127] Paradoxically he was also busy denying that he had ever wanted to leave
Ferney in the first place. The rumor had proved embarassing.

short he knew very well that it was unreasonable to stay in Paris, but he simply could not tear himself away. "Plusieurs honnêtes gens effrayées du train que prennent les choses, sont tentés de suivre le conseil que vous me donnez. Qu'ils partent, et quel que soit l'azile qu'ils auront choisi, fût ce au bout du monde, J'irai" (Best. 12719). In other words, no. Unlike Frederick, Diderot did not know how to refuse Voltaire, but it was clear that he had no intention of moving to Cleves. Voltaire could find little consolation in the fact that the La Barre affair (*le train que prennent les choses*) had been almost as persuasive as he had hoped.

Why had he asked for asylum in Cleves to begin with? "L'éxécution du chevalier *de La Barre*", assumes Wagnière, "donna quelque temps à notre philosophe une si grande horreur pour sa patrie, qu'il était sur le point de se retirer auprès de Clèves" (I, 90). The plan to establish a "philosophical" industry beyond the borders of France was definitely an attempt to derive a great benefit from a notorious evil. Because of the Abbeville atrocity, Voltaire had come closer than ever before to realizing his venerable dream, "diriger une république de *sages*" [128]. One has the impression that the other Encyclopedists, perhaps even d'Alembert, were less reluctant than Diderot, who was obviously tempted. Had Voltaire succeeded in dislodging him, an important new episode would have been added to the history of eighteenth-century French literature.

Even if the Encyclopedia had moved to Cleves, however, it would have encountered a formidable array of problems. Would the people of Cleves, for instance, have accepted such an intrusion? Would Frederick have bothered to restrain them? In 1765 his subjects in Môtiers-Travers had stoned the house of a single "antichrist" just for publishing one thin volume [129]. Frederick himself, who had never forgotten *Akakia,* could be expected to interpret his requirements of "decency" and respect for important people strictly, if not arbitrarily. As for Voltaire, the rockets he had been sending up to burst over Paris, according to his famous boast, scarcely inspired greater confidence in his docility. Even more precarious was the undecided relationship between him and Diderot. Would Voltaire have resigned himself to the merely spiritual leadership that Diderot might have been willing

---

[128] Naves, *Voltaire et l'Encyclopédie,* p. 94.

[129] Rousseau of course, whose *Lettres écrites de la montagne* had appeared the year before. Voltaire "ne se doute guère que le pélerinage le plus populaire d'une région catholique entre toutes, Kevlaar, est très proche de Moyland." Fernand Baldensperger, "un Projet voltairien," *Revue de Paris,* XLIV (avril, 1937), p. 659.

to yield to him? Would Diderot have honored the inevitable advice of a more impetuous, yet less progressive [130] "philosopher" who had relatively little experience in collaboration? On the grounds of religion alone, Diderot the materialist would have found himself at odds with Voltaire the deist. "Philosophy" itself, the supposed brotherhood that united them, had a different meaning in Paris and Ferney. Always the more realistic of the two in their dealings with each other, Diderot must have foreseen the nightmare that awaited them in Cleves.

Actually Diderot's constant reluctance to cooperate condemned all three of Voltaire's attempts to emancipate and probably appropriate the Encyclopedia. Yet Voltaire had planned and timed each attempt more carefully than the preceding one. In 1752 the *Encyclopédie* was encountering its first serious difficulties, but they would prove mild by comparison to those yet to come. Though inexperienced in such work, Voltaire was emerging as the sole contributor to the *Portatif* which he had intended as a collective work. His plan to merge with Diderot and d'Alembert apparently progressed no further than the proposal he submitted to Frederick. Even if the latter had accepted, however, it seems unlikely that Diderot would have agreed to leave Paris. In 1758 the Encyclopedists had lost their privilege to publish in France. Gex, moreover, might have offered greater freedom and security than Potsdam, especially in view of Frederick's behavior six years before. Voltaire himself could now claim limited experience in collaboration with the *Encyclopédie* in addition to the work he had done on the *Portatif*. He was also ready to take on the financial responsibility for the project himself, thus eliminating the problem of patronage. But in 1766 the last volumes of the *Encyclopédie* had appeared and the *Portatif* had been through several editions, so that the authors of both were free to dedicate themselves to the more ambitious work Voltaire had had in mind all along. Now he could boast considerable experience in encyclopedic research and writing. For the first time he had foreseen such details as the establishment of a press to print what he and his colleagues would produce. To convince them he undertook a persistent and resourceful letter-writing campaign, exploiting in particular the murder of La Barre which offered the "philosophers" a new incentive for leaving Paris. Furthermore, the Cleves project appeared to have the advantages of Fre-

---

[130] Voltaire's failure to assimilate the implications of biological discoveries exploited by Diderot is well-known.

derick's protection without the disadvantages of his presence. At last Voltaire could rightfully hope to realize his dream.

His disappointment must have been all the greater because of his determination. He seems to have been convinced that he could overwhelm the "infamous" by combining the collective talent and specialized knowledge of the *Encyclopédie* with the purpose and method of the *Portatif*. Besides, if the "brothers" did not unite under a common banner, as he warned them time and again, the enemy would crush them one by one. He saw himself as something of a prophet destined to lead the children of Philosophy from the wilderness of Superstition to the promised land of Reason. Yet he himself was the greatest obstacle to such an Exodus. However great his talents, they simply did not lend themselves to the kind of leadership he no doubt envied in Diderot.

One must not discount emulation as an important motive for his creation of the *Portatif*. He was accustomed to being admired as the greatest French writer of his times and all the evidence indicates that he enjoyed this reputation. He seems to have feared, however, that none of his own works, but rather the Encyclopedia would prove to be the most impressive intellectual monument of his century. This thought, which must have been painful to his ego, explains why he conceived the idea of the *Portatif* shortly after the Prades affair had impressed upon him the importance of the *Encyclopédie*. It also clarifies his three attempts to expatriate the project as well as his deceptively docile collaboration and eventually subversive efforts to infuse greater militance into the work. His politely scornful criticism of the *gros fatras*, especially in implied comparison to his portable dictionary, lend further support to this thesis. But his rivalry with Diderot and his collaborators never exceeded the limits of friendly, if clandestine competition. He published the *Portatif* for instance at a time when the *Encyclopédie* was underground and refrained from comparisons between the two works during his publicity campaign. The failure of his project to "reduce" the Encyclopedia in Cleves two years later led to the creation of the *Questions sur l'Encyclopédie*, likewise born of competition with the work named in its title. Except for the definitions he contributed to the Academy dictionary, all of his alphabetical writings may be ascribed in part to his desire to keep up with Diderot and company.

As for the *Portatif*, the story of its creation may be said to end in 1767 with the final edition of this title sponsored by Voltaire, even though the contents of the work would reappear in the *Raison par*

Alphabet in 1769 and then continuously in the *Dictionnaire philoso-phique* as well as the *Questions*. As usual the 1767 edition had more to offer than the preceding ones: eighteen new articles, supplementary sections for three old ones and additions to three others. Since the work had been growing less portable even before it lost its title, what really came to a close in 1767 was a curious chapter in the intellectual history of eighteenth-century Europe. The fifteen years since the inception of the project in Potsdam had not seen the dogged per-sistence of a Montesquieu writing his *Esprit des Lois* (1748), but rather a series of intermittent surges during which Voltaire's activity must have been intense. He appears to have crammed the bulk of his labor on the *Portatif* as published in 1764 into the following three periods: October-November 1752, January 1760 — January 1761 and October 1762 — January 1763. Towards the end of 1763 he may also have made a revision of the work in preparation for publication in 1764. Thus the *Portatif* survived long periods of neglect and thrived on short bursts of energy. Unlike other authors, moreover, Voltaire was not content to abandon his manuscript to a publisher and hope for news of its success. His publicity campaign in 1764 shows that the *Portatif* was not just a book, but an act as well, and its successive editions demonstrate how dynamic his concept of action could be. The cruelty of his enemies' reaction in 1766 may in fact be taken as a measure of the impact he had achieved. Although he did not slay the "monster" as he had predicted, he did deal it a wicked blow.

This "hydra", as he also called it, has of course grown other heads since the eighteenth century, yet the sword he had forged would prove almost permanently effective for lopping them off. The critical scru-tiny of "superstition", whatever form it may take, will always reveal contradictions, thus raising doubts, at which point one need only yield to the authority one has just undermined and leave obvious conclusions to public opinion. But maximum efficiency consists in reaching the greatest number with the least liability, a lesson the modern press has learned only too well. Thus the appeal to the ordinary intelligence [131] of most readers through accessibility, variety and simplicity represents considerable progress towards mass com-munication as we know it today. What really preserves the *Portatif* from the fate of other once timely attacks on now forgotten tyran-

---

[131] In this sense the *Portatif* completely eclipsed Fontenelle's explanation of certain physical sciences in terms of galantry for the benefit of the ladies in his *Entretiens sur la Pluralité des mondes* (1686).

nies of the intellect is Voltaire's use of irony as a literary tool and propaganda weapon. The work will no doubt be remembered as a dictionary of ironical comments on an institution whose respectability had worn thin.

BIBLIOGRAPHY

Jérôme Vercruysse discusses the preparation of "les Oeuvres alphabétiques de Voltaire" (*Revue de l'Université de Bruxelles*, XXII [1969—1970],
pp. 89—98) for publication in the forthcoming *Complete Works of Voltaire*. In "Un Scandale calculé" (*Voltaire et Marc Michel Rey* in *SVEC*,
LVIII, 1717—1731), he investigates the publication of the 1764 Amsterdam
edition of the *Portatif*, postdated 1765. The edition of this work edited by
Raymond Naves and Julien Benda includes the useful "Caractère de cette
édition" and "les Articles du *Dictionnaire philosophique* classés par édi-
tions". The same two authors trace the influence of some of Voltaire's more
dynamic ideas in their "En Marge d'un dictionnaire" (*Revue de Paris*,
XLIII [mars 1936], pp. 18—29). Style is the concern of Jeanne Monty in
Etude sur le style polémique de Voltaire: le Dictionnaire philosophique
(*SVEC*, XLIV), but the implications of her study overreach the boundaries
prescribed by her title. Although René Pomeau's "Histoire d'une oeuvre de
Voltaire: *le Dictionnaire philosophique portatif*" (*L'Information littéraire*,
VII [1955], 43—50) presents an interesting account, it is not as comprehensive as the title indicates and most of the indispensable *Voltaire's Correspondence* (Geneva, 1953—1965) edited by Theodore Besterman was not
available to him. In his "Voltaire's *Dictionnaire philosophique* : les Questions sur l'Encyclopédie" (*Symposium*, V [1951], pp. 317—327), William
Archie explains the relationship between the *Portatif* and the *Questions*,
with particular emphasis on the author's intentions. Ira Wade offers an
interesting but brief study of the alphabetical works in his "Genesis of the
Questions sur l'Encyclopédie" (*Transactions of the American Philosophical
Society*, New Series XLVIII [July 1958], pp. 82—85), but he tends to
consider the *Portatif* as a mere initial step in the elaboration of the *Questions*. In "la Philosophie de Voltaire d'après *le Dictionnaire philosophique*", *Synthèses* (juin-juillet 1961), Jean Cazeneuve studies ideas in general,
while André Rousseau examines" l'Idée du *progrès* dans *le Dictionnaire
philosophique*" in *Annales de la Faculté d'Aix*, XL, 65—71. And Alfred
Bingham reports "The Earliest Criticism of Voltaire's *Dictionnaire philosophique* (*SVEC*, XLVII, 15—37).

Clifford Crist not only presents an interesting, though partially obsolete
account of composition and publication in *The Dictionnaire philosophique
portatif and the Early French Deists* (Brooklyn, 1934), but also contributes
to knowledge of contemporary sources. Recently reprinted (New Haven,
1967), *Voltaire and the English Deists* by Normann Torrey answers a more
important question in a more general way. Torrey and Wade co-author
"Voltaire and Polier de Bottens" (*Romanic Review*, XXXI, 147—155)
which, like Mina Waterman's "Voltaire and Fernand Abauzit" (*Romanic*

74

Review, XXXIII, 236—249), treats Voltaire's use in the *Portatif* of borrowings from works by Swiss protestants. G. Mortimer Crist's "Voltaire, Barcochebas and the Early French Deists" (*French Review*, VI, 483—489) is a study of Polier's sources. As for French Catholic influences, Jean Deprun has found little material for his "*le Dictionnaire philosophique* et Malebranche" (*Annales de la Faculté d'Aix*, XL, 73—78). Concerning Voltaire's inclusion of certain articles written for the Encyclopedia, René Pintard's "Voltaire et l'*Encyclopédie*" (*Annales de l'Université de Paris*, XII [n° spécial], 39—56) adds very little to Naves' authoritative book by the same title (Paris, 1938), while Marta Rezler defends Voltaire s attitude towards that work from both of these critics.

Frederick Jenkins' "The Article 'Conciles': Sources and Presentation" (*French Review*, XXXI, 292—294), Alfred Bingham's excellent "Voltaire and the New Testament" (*SVEC*, XXIV, 183—218) and Gilbert Mill's unpublished dissertation "The Fidelity of Voltaire to his Biblical and Patristic Sources" (D. A. 1956, n° 752) shed light on Voltaire's subject in the *Portatif*. Elizabeth Nichols in "Dom Calmet, 'qui n'a raisonné jamais'" (*French Review*, XXXI, 296—299) and especially Arnold Ages in "Voltaire, Calmet and the Old Testament" (*SVEC*, XL, 87—187) analyze the writer's assimilation and ridicule of the Benedictine scholar's Biblical erudition. Among Ages' numerous articles on Voltaire's exploitation of Scripture, "Voltaire's Biblical Criticism: A Study in Thematic Repetitions" (*SVEC*, XXX, 205—221) is particularly useful to an understanding of the *Portatif*.

KLAUS SCHREIBER

Bibliographie laufender Bibliographien zur
romanischen Literaturwissenschaft

Ein kritischer Überblick 1960—1970

1971. 80 Seiten. Kt. DM 14.80

Sonderheft der Zeitschrift für Bibliothekswesen
und Bibliographie

Diese kritische Bestandsaufnahme untersucht die laufenden Bibliographien zur romanischen Literaturwissenschaft mit internationalem Charakter im Jahrzehnt von 1960 bis 1970. Die Beschreibung der Bibliographien wurde nach einem einheitlichen Schema angelegt, um kritische Vergleiche zu ermöglichen.

Interessenten: Romanistische Institute und Seminare, Bibliotheken, Literaturwissenschaftler.

VITTORIO KLOSTERMANN · FRANKFURT AM MAIN